BAPTISTWAY

Bible Study for Texas

The Gospel of Matthew

*Jesus As the
Fulfillment of
God's Promises*

Bill Pinson

Joe Blair

Tim Trammell

BAPTISTWAY®
Dallas, Texas

Bible Study for Texas, *Matthew: Jesus As the Fulfillment of God's Promises*

BAPTISTWAY PRESS® Management Team

Executive Director, Baptist General Convention of Texas: Charles Wade
Director, State Missions Commission: James Semple
Director, Bible Study/Discipleship Division: Bernard M. Spooner

Publishing consultant: Ross West, Positive Difference Communications
Cover and Interior Design and Production: Desktop Miracles, Inc.
Front cover photo: Texas Parks and Wildlife Department

First edition: March 2001.
ISBN: 1–931060–06–1

How to Make the Best Use of Bible Study for Texas

Whether you're the teacher or a student—

1. Start early in the week before your class meets.
2. Overview the study. Look at the table of contents, read the study introduction, and read the unit introduction for the lesson you're about to study. Try to see how each lesson relates to the unit and overall study of which it is a part.
3. Use your Bible to read and consider prayerfully the Scripture passages for the lesson. (You'll see that each writer has chosen a favorite translation for each unit. You're free to use the Bible translation you prefer and compare it with the translation chosen, of course.)
4. After reading all the Scripture passages in your Bible, then read the writer's comments. The comments are intended to be an aid to your study of the Bible.
5. Read the small articles—"sidebars"—in each lesson. They are intended to provide additional, enrichment information and inspiration and to encourage thought and application.
6. Try to answer for yourself the questions included in each lesson. They're intended to encourage further thought and application, and they can also be used in the class session itself.

If you're the teacher—

A. Do all of the things just mentioned, of course.
B. In the first session of the study, briefly overview the study by identifying with your class the date on which each lesson will be studied. Lead your class to write the date in the table of contents on page 5 and on the first page of each lesson.
C. You may want to get the enrichment teaching help that is provided in the *Baptist Standard* and/or on the Internet. Call 214–630–4571

to begin your subscription to the *Baptist Standard*. Access the Internet information by checking the the *Baptist Standard* website at http://www.baptiststandard.com or the *Bible Study for Texas* website at http://www.bgct.org/sunday_school/bstmain.htm. (Other class participants may find this information helpful, too.)

D. Get a copy of the *Teaching Guide*, which is a companion piece to these lesson comments. The teaching suggestions in the *Teaching Guide* are intended to provide practical, easy-to-use teaching suggestions that will work in your class.

E. After you've studied the Bible passage, the lesson comments, and other material, use the teaching suggestions in the *Teaching Guide* to help you develop your plan for leading your class in studying each lesson.

F. Enjoy leading your class in discovering the meaning of the Scripture passages and in applying these passages to their lives.

Matthew: Jesus As the Fulfillment of God's Promises

U N I T   5

Pointed Questions and Challenging Answers

U N I T   6

Jesus' Destiny and Ours

MATTHEW: *Jesus As the Fulfillment of God's Promises*

The Gospel of Matthew portrays Jesus as the fulfillment of God's promises in the Old Testament. These promises and their fulfillment reached to the Jewish people of Jesus' day but also beyond them to all people, even to us.

As do the other three gospels, the Gospel of Matthew approaches the most significant event in all of history—the life, ministry, crucifixion, and resurrection of Jesus—from its own unique perspective and with its own purposes in view. Matthew seeks to "interpret the theological meaning of a concrete historical event to people in a particular historical situation."[1]

As we try to learn from Matthew in this study, we do well to remember first of all that Matthew is indeed dealing with Jesus' deeds and words as "a concrete historical event." Jesus really lived, ministered, taught, died on the cross, and was resurrected.

Matthew was dealing with Jesus' works and words, though, with a specific historical situation in mind. The Gospel of Matthew was intended to speak to first-century Christians who needed to know more about what Jesus did and taught as they sought to live for him in *their* day and *their* life situation.

Who were these first-century brothers and sisters of ours? We would like to know more about them than we do. Imagine, though, what life might have been like for them. Likely they were Jews who had become Christians. These Christians lived in a Jewish world that was increasingly distancing itself from them. They were facing opposition from the Jewish leaders for their commitment to Christ. What sort of information about Jesus do you think such Christians might have needed as they lived and witnessed for Christ in such a world?

That question brings us to consider the "theological meaning"—the message—that Matthew was seeking to convey to them and from which we also can learn. Think about it. Wouldn't these early Christians have needed information about what Jesus had done and taught? Wouldn't it have been helpful in their historical situation if that information focused on Jesus as the fulfillment of God's promises in the Old Testament? There are other elements in Matthew's message, of course, but that is an important one. In Matthew 5:17, in fact, Jesus pointed out clearly his relationship to the law and the prophets of the Old Testament. He had come to fulfill them. Indeed, he had come to fulfill them in a higher way and to call people to a higher way of living.

As we study the Gospel of Matthew, we will see many ways in which Matthew evidently sought consciously and pointedly to relate Jesus' life and ministry to Judaism. He used many quotations from the Old Testament, for one thing (see 1:22–23; 2:5–6,15,17,23; 8:17; 12:18–21; 13:35). He also wove together Jesus' ministry and Old Testament themes and emphases. Perhaps a major such theme is showing how God through Jesus is extending the blessings of salvation to all people—Gentiles as well as Jews. Compare, for example, Genesis 12:1–3 and Matthew 28:18–20.

There is another quite noticeable way in which Matthew related Jesus' life and ministry to Judaism. When Jews said "the Law," they were referring to the first five books of the Bible—Genesis, Exodus, Leviticus, Numbers, and Deuteronomy. Is it merely an accident that there are five major blocks of Jesus' teaching in the Gospel of Matthew? See Matthew 5—7, 10, 13, 18, and 23—25.

This study is organized so as to let these blocks of teaching stand out. Many Bible scholars suggest that the narratives next to these blocks of teaching are meant to illustrate the main theme of the teaching in that Scripture passage. This principle of the thematic relationship of the teaching section and the narrative section next to it has guided in the design of the units in this study. The study units are intended to help students follow the contours of the structure of the Gospel of Matthew and thus come to appreciate and understand Matthew's message.

Your study of the Gospel of Matthew will be enriched greatly if you keep these thoughts about this gospel in mind. As you study the Gospel of Matthew, seek to understand first what the Scripture says and what it meant to Matthew's first readers. Then look for ways in which it applies to you, your class, and your church.

Jesus is indeed the authoritative fulfillment of God's promises to us. Have you accepted that message yourself? Are you sharing it with others?

Unit One, Getting Ready for Jesus' Ministry, consists of two lessons and deals with the events that prepared the way for Jesus' ministry. The background Scripture section dealt with is Matthew 1:1—4:16.

Unit Two, Jesus' Authority in Word and Deed, provides a two-lesson study from Matthew 4:23—9:35. Included first is a lesson from the first major discourse of Jesus in Matthew, which we know as the Sermon on the Mount (Matt. 5—7). This lesson emphasizes how Jesus taught with authority. The second lesson, from Matthew 8:1—9:35, deals with actions that show his authority.

Unit Three, Go—and Come, is a two-lesson study of Matthew 9:36—12:21 that takes its cue from the missionary discourse in Matthew 10, the second major discourse of Jesus in Matthew. The first lesson of this unit focuses on this block of instruction to the disciples as Jesus sent them out as missionaries. These teachings are introduced beginning in Matthew 9:36, and they appear in Matthew 10. The second lesson, from Matthew 11:2—12:21, identifies Jesus as God's Son and the Servant Messiah. It deals with the varying responses to Jesus and emphasizes Jesus' invitation to people to come to him.

Unit Four, Time to Decide, consists of two lessons from Matthew 13—16. The first lesson treats the third major discourse of Jesus in Matthew's Gospel. In that discourse Jesus used parables to convey his message about the kingdom of heaven. This lesson is from Matthew 13:1–52. The background passage for the second lesson is Matthew 13:53—16:28. This lesson focuses on Jesus' question to Peter about Jesus' identity, Peter's response to the question, and Jesus' teaching that followed about the nature of discipleship.

Unit Five, Pointed Questions and Challenging Answers, provides a three-lesson study from Matthew 17—25. Included first is a lesson from the fourth major discourse of Jesus in Matthew, which is in Matthew 18. This lesson emphasizes the radical manner in which commitment to Christ transforms our relationships. The second lesson in the unit, from Matthew 19—22, focuses on Matthew 19:1–15, which deals with the marriage relationship, with singleness, and with how one treats children. The background passage for the third lesson in this unit is Matthew 23—25, which contains the fifth major discourse of Jesus. The theme of judgment dominates this discourse.

Unit Six, Jesus' Destiny and Ours, is on Jesus' crucifixion and resurrection and what they mean to us. The Scripture passage for this unit is Matthew 26—28. The first lesson, from Matthew 26—27, deals with Jesus' giving his life for us. The second lesson, from Matthew 28, focuses on Jesus' resurrection and his subsequent commission to his disciples to make disciples of all people.

Additional Resources for This Study[2]

W. F. Albright and C. S. Mann. *Matthew*. The Anchor Bible. Volume 26. New York: Doubleday and Company, Inc., 1971.

William Barclay. *The Gospel of Matthew*. Volumes 1 and 2. The Daily Study Bible. Philadelphia: The Westminster Press, 1958.

Craig L. Blomberg. *Matthew*. The New American Commentary. Volume 22. Nashville: Broadman Press, 1992.

M. Eugene Boring. *The Gospel of Matthew*. The New Interpreter's Bible. Volume VIII. Nashville: Abingdon Press, 1995.

Suzanne de Dietrich. *The Gospel According to Matthew*. The Layman's Bible Commentary. Atlanta: John Knox Press, 1961.

R. T. France. *Matthew*. Tyndale New Testament Commentaries. Grand Rapids: Eerdmans Publishing Company, 1985.

David E. Garland. *Reading Matthew: A Literary and Theological Commentary on the First Gospel*. New York: Crossroad, 1995.

Archibald M. Hunter. *Interpreting the Parables*. Philadelphia: Westminster Press, 1960.

Donald Senior. *Matthew*. Abingdon New Testament Commentaries. Nashville: Abingdon Press, 1998.

Frank Stagg. *Matthew*. The Broadman Bible Commentary. Volume 8. Nashville: Broadman Press, 1969.

David Wenham. *The Parables of Jesus*. Downer's Grove, Illinois: Inter-Varsity Press, 1989.

NOTES

1. Eugene Boring, "The Gospel of Matthew," *New Interpreter's Bible* (Nashville: Abingdon Press, 1995), VIII: 89.
2. Listing a book does not imply full agreement by the writers or BAPTISTWAY® with all of its comments.

Getting Ready for Jesus' Ministry

Have you ever wondered why the New Testament contains more than one account of the life and teachings of Jesus? Every word was copied by hand on parchment. Surely having just one account would have been more efficient. But one account would not have been more effective. Each of the four gospels—Matthew, Mark, Luke, and John—provides information and insights that we need to grasp the extent of Jesus' life and teachings.

A recent event helped me understand the need for all four gospels. I had enjoyed a magnificent Texas sunset. (God does some of his best artistic work in sunsets, I believe.) In discussing the sunset with some other people, I was amazed at how differently we had "seen" the sunset. One person described it as a scientist. Another as an artist. Another as a psychologist. The experience made me aware once again of how we "see" the same event in different ways. Why? Because we are "wired" in different ways by the God who created us. What a dull world it would be if we were all alike.

God knows that we see or experience reality in different ways. Therefore the Holy Spirit led people to record the life and teachings of Jesus in different ways. These ways are not contradictory but complementary. Three of the gospels—Matthew, Mark, and Luke—record the life and teachings of Jesus in a similar pattern. They are termed the "synoptic" gospels. *Synoptic* means "to see together." Yet, as similar as they are, each has a very distinct emphasis or point of view. The Gospel of John follows a different pattern from the "synoptics." Taken as a whole they give us a wonderfully full account in ways that relate to specific points of view.

The background Scripture dealt with in this unit is Matthew 1:1—4:16. These passages set the stage for the record of the marvelous ministry of Jesus and of his teachings, which amazed those who first heard them even as they do us today.

In the first of the two lessons in this unit we will see that Jesus is indeed the fulfillment of God's promises and is "God with us" for everyone (Matthew 1:18—2:12). In the second lesson we will be reminded that the story of Jesus is not merely interesting reading but a challenge to change (3:1–17).[1]

UNIT 1: GETTING READY FOR JESUS' MINISTRY

NOTES

1. Unless otherwise indicated, all Scripture quotes in Unit 1, Lessons 1–2, are from the New International Version.

Study Aim

To identify implications of Jesus' coming as "God with us," for all people

Texas Priorities Emphasized

- Share the gospel of Jesus Christ with the people of Texas, the nation, and the world
- Develop Christian families
- Strengthen existing churches and start new congregations

Main Focus

Jesus' miraculous birth and the responses to it teach of God's special presence in him for both Jews and Gentiles—for all people.

Question to Explore

Are there any people whom God doesn't love or for whom God didn't send Jesus?

LESSON ONE

God with Us, for Everyone

Quick Read

The miraculous birth of Jesus indicates his divine nature, and the response to his birth shows that he offers salvation from sin to all people.

Have you noticed the change in the religious landscape of Texas? Once termed the "Baptist Zion," Texas has become a land of many faiths and none. People are coming to Texas from throughout the United States and from all over the world. Many of these people have little knowledge of Jesus and even less of Baptists. Christian churches exist alongside Moslem mosques, Buddhist temples, and Hindu shrines. Newspapers carry notices of Baptist revivals and of Zoroastrian feasts. This is not your grandparents' Texas!

These changes mean that Baptist Christians in Texas have a terrific opportunity to share the good news of Jesus Christ alongside a humbling challenge to do so. Each Baptist needs to be able to share with everyone everywhere who Jesus is and what he can do for people in all conditions and situations. The Gospel of Matthew will help us do that.

God with Us (1:18–25)

From the very beginning of his account Matthew wanted his readers to know who Jesus is. Matthew doesn't keep us in suspense. Neither does he try to argue why we should believe what he writes. He simply states the facts, amazing as they are.

In several ways Matthew presents facts that clearly indicate that Jesus is "God with us." Matthew begins with the genealogy of Jesus (Matthew 1:1–17). The Jewish people of Matthew's day held an official record of ancestry in high regard. Today many people trace their ancestry out of curiosity. The results may be comforting or startling but are usually of little consequence. However, in ancient Judaism the genealogy played a significant role. For example, Jewish priests were required to have an absolutely pure Jewish ancestry and Jews of less than pure Jewish ancestry were looked down on religiously and socially.

Keep in mind that Matthew was writing primarily for a Jewish readership. Thus the genealogy of Jesus was of great interest. Matthew traced the ancestry of Jesus from Abraham, the Father of Israel, to David, the most significant king of Israel, to Joseph, his earthly father. By so doing Matthew indicated that Jesus had every right to claim kingship. Some might protest that Joseph (Matt. 1:18) was not Jesus' biological father. That is true, but in Jewish law adoption established as much relationship as biological heritage. Joseph was the adopted father of Jesus. Put another way, Jesus was the

Matthew 1:18–25

18This is how the birth of Jesus Christ came about: His mother Mary was pledged to be married to Joseph, but before they came together, she was found to be with child through the Holy Spirit. 19Because Joseph her husband was a righteous man and did not want to expose her to public disgrace, he had in mind to divorce her quietly.

20But after he had considered this, an angel of the Lord appeared to him in a dream and said, "Joseph son of David, do not be afraid to take Mary home as your wife, because what is conceived in her is from the Holy Spirit. 21She will give birth to a son, and you are to give him the name Jesus, because he will save his people from their sins."

22All this took place to fulfill what the Lord had said through the prophet: 23"The virgin will be with child and will give birth to a son, and they will call him Immanuel"—which means, "God with us."

24When Joseph woke up, he did what the angel of the Lord had commanded him and took Mary home as his wife. 25But he had no union with her until she gave birth to a son. And he gave him the name Jesus.

adopted son of Joseph. Therefore, Jesus was the "Son of David," a phrase Matthew uses often (see 9:27; 12:23; 15:22; 20:30,31; 21:9,15; 22:42).

Next Matthew sets forth the fact that Jesus was both human and divine (1:18–25). His human nature came from Mary, his mother. Matthew portrays Jesus as fully human except for the fact that he did not sin. Mary gave birth to Jesus in the natural process of birthing. Jesus grew from infancy, to adolescence, to manhood. He experienced hunger, weariness, temptation, pain, and death. Jesus was not a spirit deceiving people into thinking he was a man; he was human.

Once termed the "Baptist Zion," Texas has become a land of many faiths and none.

Jesus' divine nature came from the fact that the Holy Spirit conceived him. Mary and Joseph were betrothed or engaged. When Joseph, a "righteous man" (1:19), first learned that Mary was pregnant, he considered a quiet divorce. The angel told him, however, "What is conceived in her is from the Holy Spirit" (1:20). Joseph accepted this message. He therefore did not divorce Mary but rather followed the directive of the angel. Thus Mary was a virgin when she gave birth to Jesus, who was conceived by the Holy Spirit.

If Mary and Joseph were not yet married when she became pregnant, why would Joseph consider a divorce at all? Isn't divorce for those who are

Matthew 2:1–12

[1]After Jesus was born in Bethlehem in Judea, during the time of King Herod, Magi from the east came to Jerusalem [2]and asked, "Where is the one who has been born king of the Jews? We saw his star in the east and have come to worship him."

[3]When King Herod heard this he was disturbed, and all Jerusalem with him. [4]When he had called together all the people's chief priests and teachers of the law, he asked them where the Christ was to be born. [5]"In Bethlehem in Judea," they replied, "for this is what the prophet has written:

[6] "'But you, Bethlehem, in the land of Judah,
are by no means least among the rulers of Judah;
for out of you will come a ruler
who will be the shepherd of my people Israel.'"

[7]Then Herod called the Magi secretly and found out from them the exact time the star had appeared. [8]He sent them to Bethlehem and said, "Go and make a careful search for the child. As soon as you find him, report to me, so that I too may go and worship him."

[9]After they had heard the king, they went on their way, and the star they had seen in the east went ahead of them until it stopped over the place where the child was. [10]When they saw the star, they were overjoyed. [11]On coming to the house, they saw the child with his mother Mary, and they bowed down and worshiped him. Then they opened their treasures and presented him with gifts of gold and of incense and of myrrh. [12]And having been warned in a dream not to go back to Herod, they returned to their country by another route.

married, not merely engaged? The marriage practice of the Jews in the first century explains why Matthew used the term "divorce." A marriage traditionally required three steps. The first was engagement of the couple. Parents or a matchmaker usually arranged this while the pair were children. After the couple reached some maturity, usually in the teens for the girl, unless some problem had developed the two were officially betrothed. The stage of betrothal usually lasted about a year during which time the two were expected to refrain from sexual intercourse. By the time of betrothal the union was firmly enough established that any breaking of it called for divorce. Thus Joseph considered a quiet divorce from Mary until the angel directed otherwise. The final stage was the marriage, a major public ceremony and celebration. So Joseph "took Mary home as his wife" (1:24).

Part of the directive from the angel was to name the baby "Jesus." Joseph did this. In biblical times names were of great importance, indicating something about the person who bore the name. Mary's baby was given the name "Jesus" because "he will save his people from their sins" (1:21). The name "Jesus" means "Savior."

Jesus also bore the name or title of "Christ" because he was the Messiah, the fulfillment of Old Testament prophecy. "Christ" (Greek) and "Messiah" (Hebrew) both mean "Anointed One." Matthew cites a passage from the Jewish Scriptures to show that Jesus was indeed the Anointed One promised through the centuries (1:22–23; see Isaiah 7:14). The Jews expected the Messiah to restore them to the glory enjoyed under King David. That expectation implied military might. The fact that Jesus was a descendant of David might lead the Jews to expect that Jesus would be such a Messiah. However, Matthew records that the angel indicated Jesus was not to be a military or political ruler but rather one who "will save his people from their sins" (Matt. 1:21).

> *All the facts that Matthew had set forth lead up to this staggering statement: Jesus is God with us!*

The prophecy from Isaiah also indicates that "they will call him Immanuel—which means, 'God with us'" (1:23). All the facts that Matthew had set forth lead up to this staggering statement: Jesus is God with us! The basic features of Jesus' life and ministry center in his incarnation, crucifixion, resurrection, ascension, and return. Matthew sets forth the accounts of each of these in his gospel. Here he focuses on the beginning of the incarnation—the baby conceived by the Holy Spirit and born of a virgin.

> *The incarnation is a mystery, obviously beyond human explanation or understanding. In the simplest terms, Jesus was God with flesh on his face.*

The incarnation is a mystery, obviously beyond human explanation or understanding. In the simplest terms, Jesus was God with flesh on his face. Jesus himself affirmed this amazing truth when he declared, "'Anyone who has seen me has seen the Father'" (John 14:9). And Paul, the great first century missionary-theologian, stated of Jesus: "He is the image of the invisible God . . . . For God was pleased to have all his fullness dwell in him" (Colossians 1:15,19).

Immanuel, God with us, the incarnation—whatever term you choose— sets Jesus apart from any other who has been, is, or will be, including all of

The Wise Men

Many legends have developed around the magi, or wise men, who came from the east to worship the baby Jesus. No one knows how many there were. Three is the most accepted number because there were three gifts. They have been given these names: Caspar, Melchior, and Balthasar. But no one knows what their names were.

The gifts have been given symbolic meaning: gold for a king; incense for a priest; and myrrh for the dead. Indeed Jesus was King of Kings, the Great High Priest, and he would die on the cross to save us from our sins. However, the gifts were those that would be brought to any great monarch.

What is actually known about these magi is that they overcame great obstacles of distance and politics to follow the star. So ought we to cross any barrier to follow God's will. And they came to worship him, not to speculate or debate. So should we. And they brought offerings fit for a king. So should we.

the founders of other religions. In other religions the founder says, *I will teach you the way to live.* In contrast, Jesus, God in the flesh, declares, *Follow me. I will show you the way to life abundant and eternal.* In all the other religions of the world, the word remains word. In Jesus the "Word became flesh and made his dwelling among us" (John 1:14). What a difference!

Jesus came not just for the Jews but for everyone everywhere.

Matthew's opening account reminds us that God is in control of history but also that God utilizes human instruments to carry out his will. What if there had been no families such as those of Mary and Joseph and such as the family they themselves established? God still needs families centered in his will to carry out God's work in the world today.

Matthew's Gospel contains more of the teachings of Jesus than any of the other gospels. However, Matthew clearly established that Jesus was much more than a great teacher. He was and is "God with us." The case is clear: Jesus is the fulfillment of prophecy, in the lineage of King David, conceived of the Holy Spirit, virgin born, and "God with us" to be our Savior.

For Everyone (2:1–12)

Furthermore, Jesus came not just for the Jews but for everyone everywhere. That the Messiah would be for the benefit of both Jew and

Gentile was not a new idea. The Old Testament prophecies predicted this; see, for example, Isaiah 42:6; 49:6–7. Yet most Jews in Jesus' day regarded the coming Messiah as being for them almost exclusively. Matthew shattered that concept in several ways, showing that Jesus is for everyone.

The genealogy of Jesus recorded by Matthew clearly demonstrates that God's love extends to all people. The list of people in the genealogy contains the greats of Jewish history, such as Abraham and David. It also, however, carries the names of people who were not Jews, such as Ruth, who was a Moabite (Ruth 1:4). In addition, the list contains the names of women. A rarity in

> *Jesus is the fulfillment of prophecy, in the lineage of King David, conceived of the Holy Spirit, virgin born, and "God with us" to be our Savior.*

such genealogies, this fact hints that Jesus in his ministry would elevate significantly the place of women, who were at that time regarded as little more than property. The list also indicates that God includes both "saint" and "sinner" in his love and plan. No one in the genealogy is without sin, of course, for only Jesus is sinless. Yet some of the great spiritual leaders,

William Carey and the Modern Missionary Movement

William Carey launched the modern missionary movement.[1] Carey was a Baptist cobbler and preacher in England. Today we would term him "bivocational."

In 1792, when Carey was in his early thirties, he preached a sermon at the Baptist associational meeting in Nottingham. The text was Isaiah 54:2–3, with the theme "Expect great things from God; attempt great things for God." He appealed to his fellow Baptists to undertake sharing the gospel with people of other lands.

Many rejected his appeal as being either impractical or unnecessary. Those who believed that God had determined who was to be saved or lost and that human effort made no difference used the latter argument—unnecessary. This attitude undercut evangelism and missions in Carey's day as it does in ours.

Carey pursued his vision, journeyed to India, endured great hardship, and eventually established a major mission effort there. Others followed his example, going to various parts of the world, and the modern missionary movement was launched.

such as Abraham, are listed alongside the harlot Rahab (Joshua 2:1–7) and the adulterer Bathsheba (2 Samuel 11—12).

In ways other than the genealogy, Matthew portrays God's gift in Jesus as being for all. For example, Mary and Joseph were obviously from the ranks of the common folks of their time. They were not rich or of high social standing. Jesus was born in a stable and placed in an animal feed box in Bethlehem. His birth in Bethlehem was foretold since the Messiah was to be of the line of David and Bethlehem was David's hometown (1 Samuel 16:1; 17:12; 20:6). In addition to this truth, however, it is significant that Jesus was born in a small village considered unimportant, rather than in Jerusalem, the capital and the center of political and religious life.

> Immanuel, God with us, the incarnation—whatever term you choose—sets Jesus apart from any other who has been, is, or will be, including all of the founders of other religions.

The coming of the wise men or magi from the east to worship the baby Jesus signified that "God with us" was for everyone (Matt. 2:1–12). Little is known about the wise men other than that they were from a place a great distance east of Bethlehem. They were not Jews. More than likely they were Persians. Yet they came to Jesus.

Old Testament prophecy had indicated the turning of the Gentiles to worship the God of Israel. Often people try to capture Jesus and make him be only for their culture, their race, or their part of the world. But Jesus is for everyone. The magi demonstrated that! Their coming foreshadows the Great Commission of Jesus recorded in Matthew 28:18–20.

But not everyone for whom Jesus came accepted him then, even as everyone does not accept him now. Herod, the king at Jesus' birth, feared someone would take his throne from him (2:3–12). Herod assassinated his own sons, thinking they were plotting to overthrow him. When he heard the magi say that they had come to worship the newborn King of the Jews,

A Church's Decision

A church in a neighborhood undergoing transition from Anglo to Hispanic and Black began to experience decline in membership and finances. Some of the members wanted to reach out aggressively to the newcomers in the community and encourage them to become members of the church. Others wanted to start missions or new churches for the newcomers. In light of the fact that the gospel is for everyone, what would you recommend and why?

the news terrified him. Rather than join them in adoration of the King, he determined to find the baby and kill him. Many today reject the Christ, some even attempting to eliminate all who follow him.

Calling the religious leaders and teachers together, Herod inquired where the Christ was to be born (2:4). They quoted the prophecy from Micah 5:2 indicating that Bethlehem was to be the place. Rather than be excited about the fulfillment of the prophecy, the religious leaders and teachers apparently met the news with indifference. Many in our time still meet the good news about Jesus with casual indifference. Or perhaps the religious leaders were afraid to show any real interest in the

> *The coming of the wise men or magi from the east to worship the baby Jesus signified that "God with us" was for everyone . . . .*

birth of Jesus for fear of the reaction of King Herod, who was obviously distressed by the news. Do you know of people who display little interest in Jesus because of fear of what others might say?

Your Response?

One of the sad memories I carry is from a visit to a home during a revival meeting. The pastor and I drove up to a house with the address someone had given about a prospect for the church. The house was unpainted. The yard was void of grass. A door with a torn screen slammed back and forth in the wind. Several shabbily dressed children played in the yard. The pastor looked over the situation, put the card in his pocket, and drove off. He remarked, "These are not our kind of people." The truth is that all people are God's kind of people.

In contrast, I have a wonderful memory of Forrest Feezor when he was Executive Director of the Baptist General Convention of Texas. He shared a devotional about the hands of Jesus. He described and demonstrated the praying hands, the working hands, the healing hands, and the pierced hands of Jesus. Then he said, "There is one way that you can never picture the hands of Jesus." And with that he held up his hands in rejection. He added, as he formed his hands into a posture of acceptance, "Jesus always extends his hands to welcome those who accept his invitation, 'Come unto me.'"

Jesus is "God with us" for everyone. The response to him in the first century and in all the centuries following has been varied. He has been rejected, scorned, treated with indifference, adored, worshiped, and followed as Lord. What is your response?

For those of us who worship and follow Jesus, our responsibility is to share the good news about him with everyone everywhere. We can do that through the testimony of family and individual life centered in him. We can do that through the gifts of tithes and offerings in order that the gospel can be shared throughout the world. We can do that through personal witness as we go about our daily lives and through involvement in mission ventures such as with Texas Partnerships or Mission Service Corps. We can do that as we strengthen our church and help to start new churches for everyone.

The fact that Jesus is "God with us" brings not only comfort but also a challenge to take that good news to everyone. How are you responding to this comfort and challenge?

QUESTIONS

1. How would you explain to a non-Christian who Jesus is?

2. Do you remember an incident in which someone showed you how to do something rather than merely told you how? In what way does this relate to the incarnation of Jesus?

3. How do people you know regard Jesus? As a good man? As a master teacher? As one of the best people who ever lived? As God with us? Or as some other?

4. What response do you encounter most frequently when you share the good news about Jesus? Hostility? Rejection? Tolerance? Argument? Acceptance? Or some other?

5. What purpose is served by having more than one account of the life and teachings of Jesus in the Bible?

6. In what ways can you help share the good news about Jesus with all people everywhere?

NOTES

1. Robert G. Torbet, *A History of the Baptists*, rev. ed. (Valley Forge: The Judson Press, 1963), 80–83.

Focal Text
Matthew 3:1–17

Background
Matthew 3:1—4:16

Main Focus
The gospel challenges and enables us to make a fresh start in life that is verified by changes in how we live and symbolized by Christian baptism.

Study Aim
To respond fully to God's call to change our lives

Question to Explore
How much difference does Jesus really make in your life?

Texas Priorities Emphasized
- Share the gospel of Jesus Christ with the people of Texas, the nation, and the world
- Equip people for ministry in the church and in the world

LESSON TWO

Challenged to Change

Quick Read
Challenges to change our lives come from many different sources, but the only thorough and lasting change comes through Jesus Christ. Baptism symbolizes this change.

Not long ago I took part in the baptism of our grandson Brooks. He and I had visited about his trusting Christ as his personal Savior, and he assured me that he had. Then we talked about baptism. He explained in a clear way for an eight-year-old that baptism does not save anyone from his or her sin but is a picture that we have been saved. A few weeks later I stood with Brooks and his pastor in the baptistery of his church, ready to assist in the beautiful ordinance of believer's baptism. What a thrill, I thought, to be part of something that goes all the way back to Jesus when John the Baptist baptized him! This act signifies the beginning of a new life, of a magnificent change.

And in This Corner the Challenger (3:1–6)

Perhaps no one other than Jesus has challenged people to change their lives with greater forcefulness than John the Baptist. Who was this fierce proclaimer of repentance? Why did he play such a big role in the beginning of Jesus' ministry? What was the meaning of his challenge to change? How does it relate to the life and teachings of Jesus?

In the Gospel of Matthew, John the Baptist storms suddenly out of the desert, preaching a stern message of repentance. In Luke's Gospel his birth is pictured in more tender terms but with the promise of the ministry that was to be uniquely his: to prepare the way for the Messiah.

Luke records that John's parents were Zechariah and Elizabeth. Zechariah was a priest in the temple, and Elizabeth was a relative of Mary, the mother of Jesus (Luke 1:1–80). Zechariah and Elizabeth were old and had no children. The angel Gabriel appeared to Zechariah with the promise of the birth of a son. Upon the birth of the child, Zechariah prophesied that he would be a prophet and prepare the way for the Lord (Luke 1:76). And Luke adds, "And the child grew and became strong in spirit; and he lived in the desert until he appeared publicly to Israel" (Luke 1:80).

And appear John the Baptist did, with the fury of a thunderstorm breaking over a quiet but parched land. (See also Luke 3:1–20.) He was indeed a prophet and as such shattered 400 years of prophetic silence in Israel. An ascetic, he drank no fermented beverage and ate only locusts and honey in the wilderness (Matt. 3:4; Luke 1:15). Fearless in his speech, he maintained a stern commitment to right and a rigid rejection of wrong until the end of his life when he was beheaded for daring to attack the morality of royalty (Mark 6:14–29).

Matthew 3:1–17

[1]In those days John the Baptist came, preaching in the Desert of Judea [2]and saying, "Repent, for the kingdom of heaven is near." [3]This is he who was spoken of through the prophet Isaiah:

"A voice of one calling in the desert,
    'Prepare the way for the Lord,
        make straight paths for him.'"

[4]John's clothes were made of camel's hair, and he had a leather belt around his waist. His food was locusts and wild honey. [5]People went out to him from Jerusalem and all Judea and the whole region of the Jordan. [6]Confessing their sins, they were baptized by him in the Jordan River.

[7]But when he saw many of the Pharisees and Sadducees coming to where he was baptizing, he said to them: "You brood of vipers! Who warned you to flee from the coming wrath? [8]Produce fruit in keeping with repentance. [9]And do not think you can say to yourselves, 'We have Abraham as our father.' I tell you that out of these stones God can raise up children for Abraham. [10]The ax is already at the root of the trees, and every tree that does not produce good fruit will be cut down and thrown into the fire.

[11]"I baptize you with water for repentance. But after me will come one who is more powerful than I, whose sandals I am not fit to carry. He will baptize you with the Holy Spirit and with fire. [12]His winnowing fork is in his hand, and he will clear his threshing floor, gathering his wheat into the barn and burning up the chaff with unquenchable fire."

[13]Then Jesus came from Galilee to the Jordan to be baptized by John. [14]But John tried to deter him, saying, "I need to be baptized by you, and do you come to me?"

[15]Jesus replied, "Let it be so now; it is proper for us to do this to fulfill all righteousness." Then John consented.

[16]As soon as Jesus was baptized, he went up out of the water. At that moment heaven was opened, and he saw the Spirit of God descending like a dove and lighting on him. [17]And a voice from heaven said, "This is my Son, whom I love; with him I am well pleased."

John the Baptist was the forerunner to Jesus the Messiah. John himself declared, "But after me will come one who is more powerful than I, whose sandals I am not fit to carry" (Matt. 3:11). Old Testament Scriptures declared that a special forerunner would precede the Messiah (Deuteronomy 18:18). Malachi wrote: "See, I will send you Elijah the prophet before that great and dreadful day of the Lord comes" (Malachi 4:5). John dressed much as

Elijah had dressed (2 Kings 1:8). The picture was clear; the one to herald the coming of the Messiah had arrived.

The Challenge to Change (3:7–12)

The message of the prophet John the Baptist was full of both warning and hope even as he pointed to the coming of the Messiah. John the Baptist sounded over and over the challenge for people to change their lives. He denounced evil, rebuked religious hypocrisy, and summoned his hearers to righteousness. Above all he called people to repent.

John the Baptist sounded over and over the challenge for people to change their lives.

John spared no one in his blistering preaching. He focused on those who likely least expected to be caught in the crossfire of his message, the Pharisees and Sadducees, the religious leaders of the day. "Pharisee" means "separate one." Pharisees were extremely zealous laymen in terms of legalistic religious observance. However, they often failed to live up to their own standards. John blasted their lack of humility and their hypocrisy and called for them to repent and be baptized. The Sadducees, on the other hand, were entrusted with the keeping of the temple in Jerusalem. They were prone to compromise

Repent

"Repent" is the word with which John the Baptist began his prophetic salvo (Matt. 3:1). It is also the word Jesus used as he began his ministry (4:17). Obviously this word is very important. Its basic meaning is "to turn around." It carries the idea of being deeply sorry for past actions and attitudes and turning to a new and better way. Thus repentance is not merely being remorseful over the past. It calls for an about-face and forward look to the future with a resolve to follow a new way of life.

The message of repentance of both John the Baptist and Jesus differed somewhat from that of the Old Testament because they connected repentance with the coming kingdom of God. And the message from and about Jesus differed from that of John on repentance, because faith, belief, and trust are linked with repentance. In Jesus, repentance is more than a human change of attitude and action. Coupled with faith in Jesus as "God with us," repentance results in life transformation.

with the Roman authorities (remember that Rome had conquered Israel) in order to maintain their prominent place in Jewish society.

John called them a brood of vipers fleeing from the coming wrath, like snakes slithering away from a burning field. He attacked an accepted belief that because they were Abraham's descendants they had no need of repentance. Most Jews believed that the merit of Abraham assured all of his descendants a place with God for eternity. John insisted that it was not ancestry but living by truth that was needed. He added that just as a vine or fruit tree void of produce is cut down and destroyed, so would people be cut off who did not produce fruit in keeping with repentance.

> *John insisted that it was not ancestry but living by truth that was needed.*

John the Baptist focused primarily on the one whose way he was preparing. Isaiah had prophesied of his role to prepare the way for the Lord and to make straight the road for him (Isaiah 40:3–5). In the first century, road conditions were generally terrible. Only roads on which the king traveled were relatively smooth. Whenever the king was to travel on one of these special roads, word went out to prepare the way by making it as smooth as possible. Thus John was sent to prepare the way for the King of Kings.

John declared that the one to come was more powerful than he was. Furthermore, John spoke of the coming one in terms of both a promise and a threat. The promise was that he would baptize not merely with water but with the Holy Spirit and with fire (Matt. 3:11). The prophets of old had told of the coming of the Holy Sprit in a special way (Ezekiel 36:26–27; 37:14; 39:29; Isa. 44:3; Joel 2:28). So the Jews were accustomed to such language.

The word in Hebrew for spirit is *ruach* and in Greek *pneuma*. These words mean *breath* or *wind*. In the Old Testament the Spirit is described as the agent of creation (see Genesis 1:2; see also Job 33:4; 34:14–15; Psalm 104:30). Thus the Jews who heard John's promise would have understood that the baptism by the coming one would bring a breath of new life and power like a mighty wind, resulting in a new creation. Later, those who were disciples of Jesus would understand his baptism in a similar but even more profound way.

> *John was sent to prepare the way for the King of Kings.*

What does it mean to be baptized with fire (Matt. 3:11)? Here the meaning is positive. Fire brings light, warmth, and purification. Thus the baptism by the one to come will help illumine the truth, comfort the weary, and purify the believer. Jesus used each of those concepts later in his teachings.

In addition to the positive promises related to baptism by the Holy Spirit and by fire, John the Baptist hurled a warning at his hearers (3:12). The one to come would separate the good from the bad, just as the grain is separated from the chaff by winnowing. In winnowing, a fork was used to toss both grain and chaff into the air. The heavier grain would fall to the floor to be stored, and the chaff would be

. . . Jesus by his baptism symbolized his ministry of redemption.

blown away or in some way captured to be burned. Jesus in his ministry affirmed his role as one who separates, such as sheep from goats (25:31–46) and wheat from tares (13:24–30).

The Hope of Real Change (3:13–17)

No sooner had John the Baptist described the one for whom he was preparing the way than Jesus came on the scene requesting to be baptized. John protested, saying that he should be baptized by Jesus, who was greater. But Jesus insisted, and John consented.

Why did Jesus, who was sinless, submit to baptism by John? John had been baptizing those who confessed their sins (3:6). Jesus had no sins to confess. The only answer Jesus gave was, "It is proper for us to do this to fulfill all righteousness'" (3:15).

Immersion is the only way adequately to picture the death, burial, and resurrection of Jesus and our identification with his death, burial, and resurrection.

The why of Jesus' baptism has puzzled the followers of Jesus for centuries. Many answers have been suggested.

Perhaps Jesus wanted to identify with the growing desire of the Jewish people for a closer relationship with God as indicated by their flocking to hear John and be baptized. For a Jew to be baptized as a means of confessing sin was almost unheard of. The Jews

sometimes baptized converts to Judaism. Seldom, however, would a Jew be baptized, although some observed a form of ritual washing. Remember that the typical Jew thought that being a descendant of

Baptism in Texas

The first Baptist immersion of record in the Texas Gulf of Mexico involved Gail Borden, Jr., and his wife Penelope. James Huckins, missionary of the American Baptist Home Mission Society, baptized the two in the winter of 1840, in the waters off Galveston Island, as part of the newly established First Baptist Church. The two were Baptist believers who had been in Texas for over a decade but had found no opportunity to be baptized. The opportunity came when Huckins landed on Galveston Island on January 24, 1840.[1] Borden became famous for his development of condensed milk and other inventions. The Borden Milk Company bears his name.

The early Baptists of Texas stood firmly for the importance of believer's immersion. New converts were immersed in the Gulf of Mexico, in rivers, ponds, lakes, and horse troughs—wherever water could be found. These Baptists viewed immersion as a way of symbolizing that a great change had taken place as a person had repented of sin and trusted Jesus as Savior.

Abraham guaranteed him or her a relationship with God. But suddenly Jews were swarming to the Jordan to be baptized by John upon confession of their sin. Could it be that this was a preparation for Jesus' ministry, and Jesus identified with it by baptism? Thus his baptism was a sort of initiation of his public ministry.

The suggestion that I find most inspiring is that Jesus by his baptism symbolized his ministry of redemption. By being baptized he symbolized taking upon himself the sins of the people since he had no sins to confess. Later, on the cross, he took upon himself the sins of all humankind and paid the price for those sins in an act of love and humility. To submit to baptism, an act observers would consider as repentance and confession of sin, demonstrated great humility for one who was without sin. Thus Jesus' baptism foreshadowed his death on the cross as the one who came to save us from our sins.

Baptism does not save from sin but is a symbol or picture of having been saved from sin and death to newness of life in Christ.

Questions may exist about the reasons for Jesus' baptism, but the fact and manner are clear. The very word *baptize* comes from the Greek word that means, "to immerse." John did not sprinkle or pour water over Jesus; John immersed Jesus in the Jordan River. Baptists through the centuries have insisted on immersion as the mode for baptism. Immersion is the

Baptism

Which responses express a true meaning or purpose for baptism and which a false?[2]

1. Something done in obedience to the command of Christ
2. An act that is essential for salvation
3. A symbolic means of expressing the result of repentance of sin and faith in Christ
4. A way of identifying with the death, burial, and resurrection of Jesus
5. A sacrament

only way adequately to picture the death, burial, and resurrection of Jesus and our identification with his death, burial, and resurrection. The Bible says that we are buried with Jesus and raised with him in baptism (Colossians 2:12).

Baptists also insist that baptism is only for believers. Only people who have repented of their sin and trusted in Jesus as Savior and Lord are fit subjects for baptism. Baptism does not save from sin but is a symbol or picture of having been saved from sin and death to newness of life in Christ. Baptists don't baptize babies, for example, because babies are not believers.

Appeals to repentance and righteous living may bring forth good intentions and even some changes, but what is needed is a new birth.

Following his baptism, Jesus went up out of the water, heaven opened, the Spirit of God descended like a dove, and a voice from heaven declared, "This is my beloved Son, whom I love; with him I am well pleased" (Matt. 3:17). The voice not only affirmed Jesus' ministry but also indicated something of what that ministry involved. The first part of the statement is from Psalm 2:7, a psalm applied to the Messiah. The second part is from Isaiah 42:1, which comprises a portion of the Suffering Servant passages, of which Isaiah 53 is another. This thought indicated that Jesus' ministry was to involve terrible suffering.

Our Challenge

John the Baptist issued a bold challenge to his hearers to change their lives. However, he lacked the power to bring about that change. In a sense his ministry not only prepared the way for that of Jesus but also indicated the necessity for it.

Appeals to repentance and righteous living may bring forth good intentions and even some changes, but what is needed is a new birth. John appealed for people to change their attitudes and actions, which was good. Jesus goes further, making it possible for people to become new creations, and he indwells them so that the change is from within. The indwelling Holy Spirit works with Christians to enable us to become more and more like Jesus.

This difference between outer change through human effort and total change through divine indwelling is likely why Jesus said of John, "'Yet the one who is least in the kingdom of God is greater than he'" (Luke

How much difference is Jesus really making in your life?

7:28). If you are trying to "pull yourself up by your own bootstraps," consider the invitation of Jesus to follow him and be born again, be changed from within, and become a new creation with old things passed away and all things become new. Then you will be ready to be equipped for ministry in your church and in the world. How much difference is Jesus really making in your life?

QUESTIONS

1. How are the lives, ministries, and characteristics of John the Baptist and Jesus similar? different?

2. How would you explain believer's baptism (immersion) to a person from a denomination that practices infant baptism?

3. Why do you think Jesus asked to be baptized?

4. How important do you believe baptism to be? How important do you believe immersion as the form of baptism to be? Why?

5. Why do you believe some people experience radical changes in their life when they repent and believe in Christ and some do not?

6. What indication do you see today that some people still believe that their ancestry or social standing or national origin makes them "Christian"?

NOTES

1. Harry Leon McBeth, *Texas Baptists: A Sesquicentennial History* (Dallas, Texas: BAPTISTWAY PRESS®, 1998), 29–30.
2. Baptists consider 1, 3, and 4 true.

Jesus' Authority in Word and Deed

U N I T 2

Jesus began his public ministry by establishing his authority through his unique teaching and his miraculous actions. To demonstrate his authority was a dangerous thing to do. The powers in Israel during his ministry looked with great disfavor on anyone who challenged their authority.

The Romans, for example, had conquered Israel. They required the Jews to pay taxes and obey Roman laws. Roman soldiers stationed throughout Israel enforced Roman rule by brute force when necessary. The Jews, though, were a difficult people to subject. Uprisings against Rome were not uncommon. Revolutionary leaders stirred patriotic zeal among the Jews. Not surprisingly, therefore, the Roman officials were suspicious of anyone who gathered a crowd, especially one who stirred them with speeches and wondrous works.

Rome allowed some religious freedom. The Jews were allowed to maintain their temple, synagogues, and rituals. Yet this was a troubled relationship. Rome held the religious leaders responsible for helping to keep the peace. Religious unrest could lead to civil strife. Then the boot of Rome would come down on the necks of the Jewish religious leaders, stripping the Jews of their religious activities.

The Jewish religious leaders held a certain degree of authority over the people. Jesus criticized the religious leaders—Pharisees, Scribes, Sadducees, and Priests—and ignored rules and regulations they held sacred, thus challenging their authority.

Authority also rested with the Jewish civil rulers who were nothing more than puppets of Rome. Nevertheless they enjoyed a large measure of wealth and power. Civil and religious unrest, such as that stirred by Jesus, threatened the authority and privileges of such rulers. Their power to crush apparent threats to their authority is seen in the arrest and execution of John the Baptist by Herod Antipas.

Jesus knew that his ministry would antagonize all these centers of power. He realized that rejection, suffering, and death at the hands of those with such authority would mark his way. But he also knew that a greater authority than these was his. True to his mission, he courageously displayed that authority in word and deed. The first lesson in this unit, "Live Like This," from Matthew 4:17—7:29, emphasizes how Jesus taught with authority. The second lesson, "It's Your Move Now," from Mathew 8:1—9:34, deals with actions that show his authority.[1]

UNIT 2: JESUS' AUTHORITY IN WORD AND DEED

NOTES

1. Unless otherwise indicated, all Scripture quotes in Unit 2, Lessons 3–4, are from the New International Version.

Matthew 5:17–48

Matthew 4:17—7:29

Jesus calls his followers to live by his definition of "the good life," which is far different, higher, and deeper than living by the rules devised by human culture.

To contrast Jesus' view of the good life with that of the culture of Jesus' day and the culture of our day

Question to Explore

Where did your definition of "the good life" come from, and how is it different from that of Jesus?

Texas Priorities Emphasized

- Equip people for ministry in the church and in the world
- Develop Christian families

LESSON THREE

Live Like This

Quick Read

The followers of Jesus Christ are to live by his guidelines for life, not those of our culture or our own concepts of what the "good life" is.

Materials and ideas on the "good life" and how to achieve it bombard us constantly. Television and radio programs, periodicals, books, seminars, and conferences abound, hawking ideas of success and how to reach it. The ideas of success vary greatly, from material wealth to inner peace. The ways set forth to achieve these are as varied as the goals themselves.

The followers of Christ are blessed to have an authoritative guide to life at its best—life abundant and eternal. Jesus sets forth the basic guidelines for that good life in what we usually term the Sermon on the Mount.

The Setting for the Message (4:17—5:16)

Jesus spent thirty years in quiet seclusion working in a carpenter's shop in Nazareth, supporting his mother and family. When it came time to begin his public ministry, he lost no time in establishing his authority by his teaching and actions. Following his baptism, Jesus withstood Satan's temptations in the wilderness, called together a group of disciples, and initiated his ministry of preaching, teaching, and healing. He assembled the disciples on the side of a mountain to instruct them on what was expected of them—and of us, his modern day followers.

The Gospel of Matthew focuses more on the teachings of Jesus than the other gospels do. It is not surprising therefore to find five major groupings of Jesus' teachings in Matthew's Gospel. The Sermon on the Mount is the first and the longest of these.

The setting for the sermon was spectacular, likely overlooking the Sea of Galilee. Jesus had already collected a crowd of followers through his ministry. Now he began to instruct his chosen disciples on how life is to be lived. The larger crowd was allowed to listen. The passage records that Jesus "sat down" (Matthew 5:1). Whenever a Jewish teacher, often termed a rabbi, sat to teach, that posture indicated that the discourse was not casual but official. Furthermore, the phrase "began to teach" indicates repeated, habitual action (5:2). What Jesus set forth at this time he must have repeated again and again in various ways. This was not the end of his teachings on the "good life" but rather the beginning.

Jesus launched his discourse with a series of statements on what his followers were to be. He focused first on being and attitude rather than on action. This theme is carried throughout the sermon. At the beginning he set forth what have come to be known as the Beatitudes, and in sense they are exactly that—"Be-attitudes" (5:3–12). Then he insisted that those who

Matthew 5:17–48

[17]"Do not think that I have come to abolish the Law or the Prophets; I have not come to abolish them but to fulfill them. [18]I tell you the truth, until heaven and earth disappear, not the smallest letter, not the least stroke of a pen, will by any means disappear from the Law until everything is accomplished. [19]Anyone who breaks one of the least of these commandments and teaches others to do the same will be called least in the kingdom of heaven, but whoever practices and teaches these commands will be called great in the kingdom of heaven. [20]For I tell you that unless your righteousness surpasses that of the Pharisees and the teachers of the law, you will certainly not enter the kingdom of heaven.

[21]"You have heard that it was said to the people long ago, 'Do not murder, and anyone who murders will be subject to judgment.' [22]But I tell you that anyone who is angry with his brother will be subject to judgment. Again, anyone who says to his brother, 'Raca,' is answerable to the Sanhedrin. But anyone who says, 'You fool!' will be in danger of the fire of hell.

[23]"Therefore, if you are offering your gift at the altar and there remember that your brother has something against you, [24]leave your gift there in front of the altar. First go and be reconciled to your brother; then come and offer your gift.

[25]"Settle matters quickly with your adversary who is taking you to court. Do it while you are still with him on the way, or he may hand you over to the judge, and the judge may hand you over to the officer, and you may be thrown into prison. [26]I tell you the truth, you will not get out until you have paid the last penny.

[27]"You have heard that it was said, 'Do not commit adultery.' [28]But I tell you that anyone who looks at a woman lustfully has already committed adultery with her in his heart. [29]If your right eye causes you to sin, gouge it out and throw it away. It is better for you to lose one part of your body than for your whole body to be thrown into hell. [30]And if your right hand causes you to sin, cut it off and throw it away. It is better for you to lose one part of your body than for your whole body to go into hell.

[31]"It has been said, 'Anyone who divorces his wife must give her a certificate of divorce.' [32]But I tell you that anyone who divorces his wife, except for marital unfaithfulness, causes her to become an adulteress, and anyone who marries the divorced woman commits adultery.

[33]"Again, you have heard that it was said to the people long ago, 'Do not break your oath, but keep the oaths you have made to the Lord.' [34]But I tell you, Do not swear at all: either by heaven, for it is God's throne; [35]or

by the earth, for it is his footstool; or by Jerusalem, for it is the city of the Great King. [36]And do not swear by your head, for you cannot make even one hair white or black. [37]Simply let your 'Yes' be 'Yes,' and your 'No,' 'No'; anything beyond this comes from the evil one.

[38]"You have heard that it was said, 'Eye for eye, and tooth for tooth.' [39]But I tell you, Do not resist an evil person. If someone strikes you on the right cheek, turn to him the other also. [40]And if someone wants to sue you and take your tunic, let him have your cloak as well. [41]If someone forces you to go one mile, go with him two miles. [42]Give to the one who asks you, and do not turn away from the one who wants to borrow from you.

[43]"You have heard that it was said, 'Love your neighbor and hate your enemy.' [44]But I tell you: Love your enemies and pray for those who persecute you, [45]that you may be sons of your Father in heaven. He causes his sun to rise on the evil and the good, and sends rain on the righteous and the unrighteous. [46]If you love those who love you, what reward will you get? Are not even the tax collectors doing that? [47]And if you greet only your brothers, what are you doing more than others? Do not even pagans do that? [48]Be perfect, therefore, as your heavenly Father is perfect.

follow him are to be the salt of the earth, that is, people who bring both seasoning to bland living and healing to damaged lives (5:13). His disciples are also to be the light of the world, reflecting the light of his glory and illuminating the way for those who walk in the darkness of sin and superstition (5:14–16).

A series of teachings follows that challenged the religious and secular beliefs of Jesus' day and of ours. These teachings threatened not only the prominence of many in the crowd but also their way of life. The words fell like thunderbolts. Matthew records: "When Jesus had finished saying these things, the crowds were amazed at his teaching, because he taught as one who had authority, and not as their teachers of the law" (7:28–29).

The Good Life Fulfills Rather Than Destroys the Law (5:17–20)

These verses are among the most significant and yet difficult to interpret not only in the Sermon on the Mount but also in all of Jesus' teachings. They planted the seed for what was to grow into a full-blown conflict between Jesus and the religious establishment, especially the Pharisees and the teachers of the law. His declaration about them certainly did not

win their friendship: "'For I tell you that unless your righteousness surpasses that of the Pharisees and the teachers of the law, you will certainly
not enter the kingdom of heaven'"(5:20). These words must have shocked
everyone, because the Pharisees and teachers of the law were regarded as
shoo-ins for the kingdom of heaven.

The Pharisees strictly observed the laws and rituals of Judaism. As we
noted in a previous lesson, the word "Pharisee" means "separated ones."
They sought to separate themselves from
those who did not keep fully the teachings of
the Law and the Prophets. The Pharisees
made a big show of their piety. They held
exceedingly high standards, although they
did not always live up to them. The teachers
of the law, the scribes, spent their lives inter-

*Jesus sets forth the basic
guidelines for that good life
in what we usually term the
Sermon on the Mount.*

preting the Scriptures and setting forth all sorts of rules and regulations
derived from them. From a few commandments in the Law as recorded in
Scripture, they had developed literally thousands of rules to be obeyed,
many of them petty. Obviously these teachers of the law were considered
zealous in their love for the Law and pursuit of righteousness. Yet Jesus

Concern for Family Life

Do you know why Baptists in Texas have been known for their strong opposition to card playing, dancing, smoking, drinking alcohol, and gambling? Some
people think that such an emphasis is legalistic and narrow-minded. The fact is
that condemnation of these practices stems from a strong Baptist concern for
family life and social stability.

In frontier Texas, the center of the town was often the open saloon. The
saloon offered men gambling, usually by cards; alcohol; and prostitutes who
danced with the men as a means of enticing them to "go upstairs" for sexual
intercourse. Obviously these practices undermined family life and often led to
fights and even killings.

As more and more women moved west, marriage and family life became
more common. Out of concern for family stability, preachers attacked the practices in the saloons. Even after the open saloon became either extinct or of lesser
importance, preachers kept on condemning these practices. In light of what is
happening in Texas today do you believe that such preaching and teaching
should continue?

said that their righteousness along with that of the Pharisees fell short of what was expected.

Perhaps even more serious than Jesus' attack on the Pharisees and scribes was his apparent attack on the Law. He said that he had come to fulfill the Law, but he appeared to break the Law. Certainly he violated such matters as rules and regulations about Sabbath observance and ceremonial washing. How can such an apparent contradiction be explained?

One explanation rests in an understanding of what was meant by "the law." In Jesus' day the "law" had several meanings. It could refer (1) to the Ten Commandments, (2) to the first five books of the Old Testament (termed the Pentateuch or five rolls or scrolls), or (3) to the scribal laws, the multiple rules and regulations set forth by the scribes. Most of the Jews in Jesus day likely thought of the "law" in terms of the latter. (I have not capitalized "law" when referring to the latter, the scribal laws.)

So what did Jesus mean when he said that he had come not to destroy but to fulfill the Law? He obviously had not come to defend or fulfill the scribal law. He referred to the Scriptural Law as given by God. Of this Law Jesus declared that not one letter or the smallest stroke of the pen would pass away "until everything is accomplished" (5:18). He insisted that people should keep and teach the Law, but only as it is properly understood.

Jesus taught that the "good life" does not consist of merely keeping the least of the commandments. This is external righteousness. Jesus taught that people really kept the Law when they had reverence for God and respect for human beings. As he stated later when asked what was the greatest commandment in the Law: "'Love the Lord your God with all your heart and with all your soul and with all your mind.' This is the first and greatest commandment. And the second is like it: 'Love your neighbor as yourself.' All the Law and Prophets hang on these two commandments" (22:37–40). In this answer Jesus quoted from the Law (see Deuteronomy 6:5; Leviticus 19:18).

Shall I Sue?

A woman who has been wronged in a business transaction is urged to sue the offending party. She resists the possibility of a lawsuit, citing Jesus' teaching about agreeing with your adversary and not going to court. She insists that Christians ought not to settle disputes in court. Do you agree or disagree? Why?

The religious leaders and even the general population of Jesus' day seemed to think of religion in terms of following certain rules, regulations, and ceremonies. While Jesus did not advocate discarding all of these, he did indicate that the Law was fulfilled in inner attitude and changed life, not in these externals.

Jesus launched his discourse with a series of statements on what his followers were to be.

Do you know anyone today who seems to believe that religion consists of a list of *do's* and *don'ts*, with an emphasis on the *don'ts?* Jesus did not focus on religion as such but on the relationship of people to God and to one another, beginning with attitude that results in right conduct.

The Good Life Through the Law Fulfilled (5:21–48)

Jesus followed his discussion about fulfilling the Law with six illustrations of the higher righteousness he had mentioned (5:20). Each of these points beyond external action to internal attitude as the basis of the good life.

Jesus presented these illustrations in a way that amazed his listeners. Other rabbis and teachers always taught by buttressing their comments with quotations from religious authorities or Scriptures. Jesus cited neither. Rather he referred to a teaching from the Law and then stated how it should be fulfilled or carried out. He simply said, *This is what has been said in the Law, but this is what I tell you to be and to do.* Jesus' words must have been met either by stunned silence or by bewildered murmuring, such as, *We have never heard anyone like this before!*

Jesus taught that people really kept the Law when they had reverence for God and respect for human beings.

In the six illustrations Jesus emphasized thoughts or desires. Out of these flow actions. Therefore, only God can judge us because only God knows our thoughts. And since no one is free from lack of reverence for God and lack of respect for other people (the essence of the Law), we are all guilty before God. Correctly understood, the Law not only sets the standard but also establishes our sin and guilt. Since no one can live up to the standard of the Law when truly understood, everyone stands in need of forgiveness, which only God can provide. If the people listened with any spiritual perception whatever, they would have realized

that the scribal law was off base and that even the real Law needed fulfillment. That is, its meaning needed to be filled up.

In the first of the six illustrations Jesus cited the Law on murder from
Exodus 20:13. He declared that it is not enough to refrain from actual
murder (Matt. 5:21–26). A person is also to refrain from the attitude that
leads to the outer action of murder: anger. Jesus spoke of three kinds of
anger. One is brooding, selfish anger over a personal affront. A second is
contempt expressed for another by use of the term "raca." And finally
there is anger expressed by casting aspersion on the moral character of
another by calling him or her a "fool," thus destroying another's name and
reputation. By these teachings Jesus indicated that anger can lead not only
to taking another's life but also another's self-esteem or good name. Jesus
declared that a right relationship with another is destroyed by anger.
Anger is a major matter because a person cannot be right with God unless
he or she is right with other people (5:23–24). Thus it is important to settle immediately any breach between people before the division widens,
such as between two people who are headed toward litigation (5:25–26).

The second illustration deals with adultery (5:27–30). Jesus stressed
that not only the action but also the thought makes a person guilty in the
sight of God. He implied that the inner
thought is prelude to outer action. The "look"
in Jesus' teaching is one that intends to incite
lustful desire, an attitude that may well lead
to immoral sexual action. The object of such
a look may be a picture or a person. The rem-
edy Jesus mentioned is in the form of hyper-
bole, an exaggeration to make a point. He
does not intend that eyes be literally gouged
out, though some super zealous people have done this. Rather he intends
for people to remove whatever leads to lustful thoughts.

> . . . When we invite Jesus by faith into our lives, he begins to provide the direction and power to make the impossible possible.

The third illustration focuses on divorce (5:31–32). The Jewish ideal
for marriage was very high but the practice very low. Quick, easy divorce
was undermining marriage and family. There were two main schools of
thought about the meaning of the Old Testament teaching about divorce.
One insisted that only unchastity was grounds for divorce. The other
allowed divorce for almost anything about a wife that displeased her husband. The right of divorce rested almost exclusively with the husband.
Jesus held that God's ideal for the fulfillment of marriage does not include

divorce. People ought not enter marriage thinking that if it does not work out they can simply divorce and move on to another relationship.

The fourth illustration deals with oaths (5:33–37). Jesus did not cite a specific Scripture about oaths, but several Old Testament passages relate to oaths (see Exodus 20:7; Deuteronomy 23:22; Numbers 30:2–15). The Jews in Jesus' day used oaths with "mental reservations," often swearing to one thing while mentally holding to another. A clever technique of evasion was developed in which a person could swear by anything but God and the oath would not be binding. Thus Jesus said to avoid such superfluous oaths and let "yes" be "yes" and "no" be "no" without any mental reservation.

Jesus' words must have been met either by stunned silence or by bewildered murmuring . . . .

An eye for an eye, the fifth illustration (Matt. 5:38–42), is a direct statement from the Law (Exod. 21:23–25; Lev. 24:19–20; Deut.19: 21). The idea of an eye for an eye was actually a step toward mercy, putting a limit on vengeance. Jesus declared that a legalistic interpretation falls short of God's ideal for the "good life." People should always go beyond what is required or expected of them, such as accepting insult and never resenting it or returning it.

Jesus illustrated this concept in three ways. Most Jews had several tunics but only one cloak. Jesus taught that if a tunic were demanded, cheerfully give up your cloak. Roman soldiers could require Jewish subjects to carry their packs a mile. Jesus taught that if you were required to carry the pack a mile, cheerfully carry it two. Alms were part of the Jewish legal requirements. Jesus taught that if you were asked for something, cheerfully give more than is expected. In each case an attitude of going beyond what is expected is the key to the "good life."

Thus the challenge of Jesus to be perfect as God is perfect challenges us to love as God loves—all people, even those who reject and despise him.

Love for enemies is the final illustration (Matt. 5:43–48). The New Testament has more than one Greek word that is translated love. In this case Jesus used a form of the word *agape*, the highest form of love, the kind of love God has for us. Thus the challenge of Jesus to be perfect as God is perfect challenges us to love as God loves—all people, even those who reject and despise him.

An Impossible Possibility

The Sermon on the Mount provides the guide to the "good life." But to most of us it seems impossible to follow. Thus it is an impossible possibility. Jesus sets it forth as possible; we view it as impossible. Indeed, it is impossible to live up to Jesus' teachings on our own. But with God all things are possible.

Therefore when we invite Jesus by faith into our lives, he begins to provide the direction and power to make the impossible possible. As Paul declared, "I can do everything through him who gives me strength" (Philippians 4:13).

Those who first heard these words of Jesus must have thought, *We can never live up to this.* Later they were to learn how they could, even as we know and can therefore share with others the way to the "good life."

QUESTIONS

1. Why did the people who heard Jesus think that he spoke with unusual authority?

2. Why did Jesus teach that inner attitudes and thoughts are more basic to the "good life" than outer action and conduct?

3. With divorce rates high and family life threatened, how would you apply the teachings of Jesus to these problems?

4. Given the loose attitude toward sexual relations outside of marriage today, what should be the Christian's attitude toward pornography and sexually explicit movies and television? How could these relate to adultery?

5. How do you believe Jesus' teachings on oaths should be applied today?

6. What do you think Jesus meant by his statement, "Be perfect, therefore, as your heavenly Father is perfect" (5:48)?

Focal Text
Matthew 9:18–35

Background
Matthew 8:1—9:35

Main Focus
Jesus' authoritative words and deeds invite us to respond to him in faith.

Study Aim
To respond to Jesus in faith myself and identify ways of helping others respond to Jesus in faith

Question to Explore
How will you respond to Jesus' authoritative words and deeds?

Texas Priorities Emphasized
- Share the gospel of Jesus Christ with the people of Texas, the nation, and the world
- Minister to human needs in the name of Jesus Christ
- Equip people for ministry in the church and in the world

LESSON FOUR

It's Your Move Now

Quick Read
The authoritative words and deeds of Jesus should cause us to respond to his invitation to respond to him in faith and discipleship.

45

A group of students from universities throughout Texas had gathered for a retreat that included international students, many of them non-Christians. During the opening sharing session, one girl said, "I am a Baptist. I was born in a Baptist home, grew up in a Baptist church, and am active in a Baptist church now. Nobody here is going to change my mind." With her position firmly declared, she listened as others shared. At the last meeting of the retreat a brilliant post-graduate student from India said, "I am a Hindu. I have enjoyed listening to all the ways people here have found God. I believe that there is one God but there are many ways to him. Each of us should sincerely find our own way to God." The girl blurted out, "That's exactly what I believe too!" What do you think about her reaction?

True Baptists believe in religious freedom—the freedom of everyone to believe or not to believe. However, true Baptists also believe in sharing Jesus as the only true way to God and thus the way to abundant and eternal life. In this week's study Matthew sets forth the actions of Jesus that demonstrate his divine authority and that invite faith and followship.

Jesus Raises a Girl from the Dead (9:18–19,23–26)

Matthew records a series of miraculous works of Jesus that established his authority. These followed the Sermon on the Mount in which his words established his authority (Matthew 7:28–29). Jesus made lame legs walk, blind eyes see, still tongues talk, and paralyzed bodies whole. He stilled a storm on the lake. All of these mighty acts affirmed his divine authority.

Furthermore, Jesus' loving authority extended to a mosaic of people who experienced his healing touch. Included were a Roman soldier, a Jewish religious leader, a poor woman, the mother-in-law of his disciple Peter, crazed men in the wilderness, and people in the city. Some of his mighty acts included breaking down the walls of prejudice that separated people, such as his calling of Matthew, a tax collector, to be his disciple. The size and excitement of the crowds grew as Jesus performed miracle after miracle.

Each miracle met a human need. None was a mere demonstration of divine power. Following the example of Jesus, Texas Baptists maintain a priority of caring for human need in Jesus name.

The raising to life of a dead girl was one of the most impressive miracles. Her father was a "ruler" (9:18). From the account of this incident in

46

Matthew 9:18–35

18While he was saying this, a ruler came and knelt before him and said, "My daughter has just died. But come and put your hand on her, and she will live." 19Jesus got up and went with him, and so did his disciples.

20Just then a woman who had been subject to bleeding for twelve years came up behind him and touched the edge of his cloak. 21She said to herself, "If I only touch his cloak, I will be healed."

22Jesus turned and saw her. "Take heart, daughter," he said, "your faith has healed you." And the woman was healed from that moment.

23When Jesus entered the ruler's house and saw the flute players and the noisy crowd, 24he said, "Go away. The girl is not dead but asleep." But they laughed at him. 25After the crowd had been put outside, he went in and took the girl by the hand, and she got up. 26News of this spread through all that region.

27As Jesus went on from there, two blind men followed him, calling out, "Have mercy on us, Son of David!"

28When he had gone indoors, the blind men came to him, and he asked them, "Do you believe that I am able to do this?"

"Yes, Lord," they replied.

29Then he touched their eyes and said, "According to your faith will it be done to you"; 30and their sight was restored. Jesus warned them sternly, "See that no one knows about this." 31But they went out and spread the news about him all over that region.

32While they were going out, a man who was demon-possessed and could not talk was brought to Jesus. 33And when the demon was driven out, the man who had been mute spoke. The crowd was amazed and said, "Nothing like this has ever been seen in Israel."

34But the Pharisees said, "It is by the prince of demons that he drives out demons."

35Jesus went through all the towns and villages, teaching in their synagogues, preaching the good news of the kingdom and healing every disease and sickness.

Mark's Gospel we know that he was a ruler in the synagogue (Mark 5:21–43). As such he was responsible for the maintenance and services of the place where the Jews gathered for religious instruction and worship. In such a position he likely had developed an enmity for Jesus because Jesus did not observe all the rules and regulations expected of a devout Jew. Nevertheless, after trying every other source to regain life for his daughter, he turned to Jesus for help. Jesus' response demonstrates how well the

Teacher followed his own teachings. He had taught that we are to love and pray for our enemies. Here was an enemy of Jesus. Instead of rejecting the man, Jesus "turned the other cheek" and helped him by raising his daughter from death.

Some have questioned whether the girl was actually dead or in a coma. Jesus said, "The girl is not dead but asleep" (Matt. 9:24). In the warm climate where the incident took place, people were buried very soon after death because the body decomposed rapidly.

True Baptists believe in religious freedom—the freedom of everyone to believe or not to believe.

It was not uncommon for people in a cataleptic state, appearing to be dead, to be buried alive accidentally. If she were in a coma, Jesus saved her from a horrible death. However, the evidence points to her being actually dead. The word "sleep" is used for death in other passages, such as 1 Thessalonians 5:10. Furthermore, news about a girl brought back from a coma would not have been "spread through all that region" (Matt. 9:26).

Bringing the dead to life was a sign of God's omnipotence and of the coming time when death will be no more (see 1 Corinthians 15:54–57; Revelation 21:4). By this mighty act Jesus demonstrated divine authority over death, a fact that he was to demonstrate even more wonderfully in his own resurrection.

Jesus Heals a Chronically Ill Woman (9:20–22)

On his way to the house of the dead girl, Jesus healed a woman who had been chronically ill for twelve years. At first this miracle seems to pale in comparison to raising the dead, but it demonstrates the concern Jesus displayed for the total person: physical, emotional, social, and religious. His authority extends to all aspects of life.

The woman had been ill for a dozen years. Her disease caused her great discomfort, not only physical but also emotional, social, and religious. She no doubt had been to every physician and healer available. None had helped her. But, she thought, perhaps Jesus could cure her. The news of his amazing healing power had attracted a large crowd. She was in the crowd, walking behind him as he moved toward the home of the dead girl.

In a daring act of faith, the woman reached out and touched the tassel on Jesus' garment. Jesus turned and looked at her. How her heart must have pounded. What would he say! What would the crowd do! In an act of love he singled her out from the mob and said simply, "Your faith has healed you" (Matt. 9:22). The physical agony that had plagued her for a dozen years disappeared instantly.

With the physical healing came other healing. She had suffered emotionally. As anyone who has suffered chronic illness knows, the hope for cure dashed again and again by failure creates an emotional nightmare. Her illness also caused her to be a social outcast, which compounded her emotional difficulties. According to Jewish Law, spelled out explicitly in Leviticus 15:25–27, her bleeding caused her to be ceremonially unclean. She was a social and religious outcast. Added to pain, dashed hopes, and humiliation was isolation. She was not even supposed to be in

. . . True Baptists also believe in sharing Jesus as the only true way to God and thus the way to abundant and eternal life.

the crowd because anyone she touched also became unclean according to Jewish belief. Jesus did not indicate the nature of her illness because to have done so would have brought the wrath of the crowd on her. How sensitive Jesus is to our fragile human nature!

Jesus Restores Sight to the Blind (9:27–31)

The miracles of Jesus came in rapid succession. Without a lull he moved from raising the dead girl to restoring sight to two blind men. As he walked from the girl's house, two blind men followed him, calling out, "Have mercy on us, Son of David!'" (Matt. 9: 27). This was the first time the title "Son of David" had been bestowed on Jesus publicly. The account of Jesus' birth, which contains his genealogy, clearly established him as the Son of David, a messianic term (1:1). Up until the plea of the blind men, however, no one had used the title for Jesus. Later it was used several times by people crying out for help (15:22; 20:30–31).

By this mighty act Jesus demonstrated divine authority over death, a fact that he was to demonstrate even more wonderfully in his own resurrection.

Most significantly it was the title shouted by the crowd when he entered Jerusalem shortly before his crucifixion and resurrection (21:4–11).

The cry, "Son of David," may have been the reason Jesus took the men indoors away from the crowd. The healing they desired was a messianic sign described by Isaiah: "In that day the deaf will hear the words of the scroll, and out of gloom and darkness the eyes of the blind will see"(Isaiah 29:18). A little while after this event when the disciples of John the Baptist asked Jesus whether he were the Messiah, Jesus replied by telling them to report to John that "the blind receive sight" (Matt. 11:5). The combination of the cry "Son of David" and the messianic sign of healing the blind made this a very special miracle.

Shouldn't those of us who know of Jesus' love and power be bringing people to him?

Jesus was not ready, apparently, for his messiahship to be announced. He was establishing his authority by word and deed, but he wanted to make sure that people understood the nature of his messiahship. The popular idea of the messiah as the Son of David was of a ruler who would restore the glory of Israel and throw off the boot of Roman oppression. Most thought this person would be a military leader. Jesus was not to be such a leader. Rather he was the Suffering Servant who would suffer a criminal's death on a cross for the sins of the world. A correct understanding of who Jesus is helps equip people for ministry in churches and in the world, a Texas Baptist priority.

Jesus healed the two blind men but warned them sternly, "'See that no one knows about this'" (9:30). If they told of their sight being restored by the Son of David, many people would make the connection between

Miracles

Many people today have difficulty accepting miracles. With the advent of modern science and materialistic views about the physical world, a large number of people consider belief in miracles as a carryover from the pre-scientific era. However, those who accept the truth of the Bible accept these as facts.

Because the Bible does not explain miracles, it is not surprising that Christians hold various views about them. For example, they don't agree on how or why miracles occur. Some believe that miracles are part of the laws of nature, which God controls. Others contend that miracles are God's interruptions of natural processes in which he breaks in with something totally different.

As to the why of miracles, some Christians insist that they are an aid to faith or the result of faith. Others believe that faith should not be based on the miraculous except the incarnation, crucifixion, and resurrection of Jesus. The main thing to keep in mind is that God is in control.

Jesus and the prophecies concerning the coming Messiah before he had opportunity to clarify the nature of his mission.

The blind men did as multitudes after them have done: they disobeyed Jesus (9:31). For people to receive a blessing from God and then disobey his commands is not uncommon even today, is it?

Jesus Gives Speech to a Man Who Was Mute (9:32–34)

We do not know who the people were who brought the man to Jesus, but they obviously believed Jesus could heal him. Shouldn't those of us who know of Jesus' love and power be bringing people to him? How tragic that many perish because no one brings them to Jesus.

In these numerous miraculous acts, Jesus demonstrated his power and authority over disease, death, storms, and demons.

The healing of the man who was mute demonstrated the power and authority of Jesus over demons. The Bible tells us little about demons other than that they were regarded as being under the authority of the prince of demons, that is, Satan. Demons are represented as being behind certain human diseases and malfunctions. In the wilderness, Jesus resisted the temptations of the Devil. Now he showed that he had power to overcome the emissaries of the Devil. Later Jesus told his disciples that his casting out of devils showed that the kingdom of God had come to his hearers (12:23–27).

In these numerous miraculous acts, Jesus demonstrated his power and authority over disease, death, storms, and demons. He also showed that his ministry was not limited to Jews because a Roman soldier's servant experienced Jesus' power and love. Neither would Jesus allow the enmity of Jewish leaders to stand in the way of his caring for them; he restored to life the daughter of a ruler of a synagogue.

Jesus has taught and acted. Now it is our move.

The miracles of Jesus have raised many questions. For example, what is the relation of faith and miracle? So-called faith healers in our day often make a connection between faith and a healing miracle. Is faith necessary for a miracle? What sort of faith? Whose faith? Although the Bible does not provide answers to all questions about faith and miracles, the events in Jesus' life indicate that there is a close relation between the two. Jesus told the woman healed of an issue of blood, "'Your faith has healed you'" (9:22). In some instances the faith of people other than the one receiving the miraculous blessing is mentioned. Yet in the case of the mute man no mention of faith is recorded.

In pondering the relation of faith and miracle, keep in mind that the purpose of a miracle of Jesus was not primarily to demonstrate a person's faith but rather Jesus' authority. The miracles were signs of the Messiah and indications that the kingdom of God was at hand.

What about all the other people with needs who did not receive the benefit of a miracle from Jesus? Were the only ones with faith those mentioned in the accounts of miracles? That does not seem likely. And what about all of the people today who have faith in Jesus but do not experience a miracle of healing?

> In pondering the relation of faith and miracle, keep in mind that the purpose of a miracle of Jesus was not primarily to demonstrate a person's faith but rather Jesus' authority.

Shouldn't we always remember that the greatest miracle of Jesus is the incarnation, crucifixion, and resurrection and that the greatest miracle any of us can ever experience is being forgiven of our sin through faith in Jesus as Lord and Savior? After all, every one who experienced a miracle of physical healing ultimately died, but Jesus promises that those who believe in him as Savior and Lord will never die (John 11:23–26).

Responses to Jesus

Jesus demonstrated his divine authority in both his teaching and his actions. And what was the reaction to this? People chose to respond in various ways to Jesus in his day as they do in ours. Some showed by their actions that they had an inadequate understanding of who Jesus was. For example, the woman with an issue of blood seemed to have an almost superstitious approach to Jesus, believing that a touch of his garment was all that she needed. Her approach seems similar to that of people today who use items blessed by so-called holy men for healing. The blind men with their cry "Son of David" revealed an inaccurate picture of Jesus as a military savior.

Other people responded to Jesus in very negative ways. The mourning crowd at the home of the dead girl laughed at him; some people today still laugh at the teachings and claims of Jesus. The townspeople where Jesus cast demons from two men pleaded with him "to leave their region" (Matt. 8:34). Some reacted to Jesus with criticism. The Pharisees were highly critical of Jesus' association with tax collectors and sinners. The Pharisees later ascribed his mighty work of casting out demons to the prince of demons, indicating that Jesus was himself evil (9:34). The teachers of the law said to themselves, "'This fellow is blaspheming'" (9:3).

Shouldn't we always remember that the greatest miracle of Jesus is the incarnation, crucifixion, and resurrection and that the greatest miracle any of us can ever experience is being forgiven of our sin through faith in Jesus as Lord and Savior?

Still many responded in very positive ways. Matthew records: "The crowd was amazed and said, 'Nothing like this has ever been seen in Israel'" (9:33). The disciples in the boat when Jesus stilled the storm "were amazed" (8:27). Jesus recognized that much of the adoration was shallow and warned the people about the cost of following him (8:18–22). Is inadequate discipleship uncommon today?

Regardless of the reaction to Jesus' miraculous acts, no one doubted that they were real. Although the people who observed them did not fully understand who Jesus was, they realized from both his teachings and his actions that he was one with great authority. We know that authority came from God because he was "God with us."

Jesus has taught and acted. Now it is our move. To respond to such amazing facts with a shrug or a yawn is totally inappropriate. What is called for is faith and action. Will you respond to him with saving faith? Will you also share the wonderful good news about him with others?

QUESTIONS

1. In what ways did Jesus demonstrate his divine authority?

2. How have you responded to Jesus?

3. What do you think the relationship is of faith and miraculous events, such as physical healing?

4. What do you believe about demons and demon possession?

5. How do you explain the fact that of all the sick people surrounding Jesus he only healed a few?

Go—and Come

U N I T

3

This unit is a two-lesson study of Matthew 9:36—12:21. The unit takes its cue from the missionary discourse in Matthew 10. Matthew 10 contains the second major discourse in Matthew.

The first lesson of this unit focuses on the block of instruction to the disciples as Jesus sent them out as missionaries. The scene for these teachings is set beginning in Matthew 9:36, and the teachings themselves are given in Matthew 10.

The second lesson, from Matthew 11:2—12:21, identifies Jesus as God's Son and the Servant Messiah. It deals with the varying responses to Jesus and emphasizes Jesus' invitation to people to come to him.[1]

UNIT 3: GO—AND COME

Lesson 5 Commanded to Go	Matthew 9:36—10:1,5–10,24–39
Lesson 6 Invited to Come	Matthew 11:2–6,16–30; 12:15–21

NOTES

1. Unless otherwise indicated, all Scripture quotes in Unit 3, Lessons 5–6, are from the New Revised Standard Version.

Main Focus

Jesus' disciples are to respond to his call and go out in his authority to do his work, trusting fully in him.

Question to Explore

How do the actions of your life compare to the kind of life to which Jesus sent his disciples?

Texas Priorities Emphasized

- Share the gospel of Jesus Christ with the people of Texas, the nation, and the world
- Minister to human needs in the name of Jesus Christ
- Equip people for ministry in the church and in the world
- Develop Christian families
- Strengthen existing churches and start new congregations

LESSON FIVE

Commanded to Go

Quick Read

As Jesus sends out his disciples to witness to God's deliverance in Christ, so he sends us out to witness.

The church prepared for the revival. They invited, they prayed, and they visited. They borrowed one of the large rooms in a public school across the street. The young people and children of a certain age met there for a special service. The preacher presented an impassioned witness to Christ. He called for the decision to accept Christ as Lord, to which several responded. I was one of those among the pre-teens who responded. The church by its witness was going into world as Christ commanded (Matthew 28:19), and I was one of those reached by their witness.

A seminary professor recalled a revival he remembered vividly. They had consecutive services for several days. Afterward, people said, "We had only two boys saved during this revival." "But," the professor said to us, "I was one of those boys."

The mission of the church is that of carrying out the mission of Jesus. When we read the biblical text, such as in Matthew 9:35, we see Jesus going: "Then Jesus went about all the cities and villages, teaching in their synagogues, and proclaiming the good news of the kingdom, and curing every disease and every sickness." Jesus was on a mission of deliverance, and he called his apostles to mission as well.

Go in Compassion and Authority (9:36—10:1)

Jesus saw with compassion a people desperately in need of deliverance. They were "harassed and helpless, like sheep without a shepherd" (9:36). This picture evoked his compassion. *Compassion* is a strong word describing feelings that we might identify with the word *pity*. They were people who had an aimless and futile existence. They were lost, just as people today apart from Jesus, the shepherd, are lost.

But the people could be reached. They were a harvest waiting for the workers. Whenever the Messiah came, he was to gather in the people of God into the kingdom, into the rule of God. The kingdom had arrived in Jesus, and he was eager to gather in his people. The task was big. The need for workers was great. The "Lord of the harvest" (9:38), however, could meet that need. In an actual harvest, the "chief harvester" was like a foreman or manager. His responsibilities included hiring workers. Obviously, Jesus referred to himself. He sends the workers into the harvest, and success will attend the harvesting because the harvest is "plentiful" (9:37).

The workers in this case were the "twelve disciples" (10:1). Already they had been with Jesus. He prepared them during that period. While

Matthew 9:36–38

[36]When he saw the crowds, he had compassion for them, because they were harassed and helpless, like sheep without a shepherd. [37]Then he said to his disciples, "The harvest is plentiful, but the laborers are few; [38]therefore ask the Lord of the harvest to send out laborers into his harvest."

their time of preparation was not over, Jesus considered them ready for the assignment. Jesus added to the equipping already done by granting authority to them to cast out "unclean spirits" and heal diseases and sickness (10:1). Jesus commanded them to go under his authority and compassion, doing the same ministry that he did. The healing events and the casting out of evil were signs that with Jesus God's kingdom (rule) had broken into people's lives, and thus into history, in a special way.

Going out as Jesus commands and equips results in human wholeness. Jesus' ministry made people whole as he delivered them from evil, disease, and sickness. Responding to and receiving the rule of God in life gave people wholeness.

The mission of the church is that of carrying out the mission of Jesus

The church participates in Jesus' ministry today as it goes to the harvest under the call of Christ. The church sees people delivered from evil, people getting well, broken relationships mended, and other manifestations of wholeness. Much happens that we do not see. Sometimes we pray for a person to be well from an illness or disease and the physical sickness persists. But we see the person enabled to cope and accept. We see the light of truth and faith conquer fear and discouragement. Hopelessness is dispelled; wholeness results.

A friend, a church member to whom the church ministered, entered the hospital. His illness did not appear life threatening, and we expected him to return home soon. He remarked as his illness persisted, "I am not afraid of death. Everything is right with me. I have had a wonderful life. I have lived through the best times." In this man's courage we see a miracle although the illness did not go away. Of course, there are times when we see both miracles happen.

The church sent out under the authority and compassion of Christ today can go in confidence. Wholeness in peoples' lives results from Christ's ministry in and through his disciples, the church.

Matthew 10:1,5–10,24–39

[1]Then Jesus summoned his twelve disciples and gave them authority over unclean spirits, to cast them out, and to cure every disease and every sickness.

• •

[5]These twelve Jesus sent out with the following instructions: "Go nowhere among the Gentiles, and enter no town of the Samaritans, [6]but go rather to the lost sheep of the house of Israel. [7]As you go, proclaim the good news, 'The kingdom of heaven has come near.' [8]Cure the sick, raise the dead, cleanse the lepers, cast out demons. You received without payment; give without payment. [9]Take no gold, or silver, or copper in your belts, [10]no bag for your journey, or two tunics, or sandals, or a staff; for laborers deserve their food.

• •

[24]"A disciple is not above the teacher, nor a slave above the master; [25]it is enough for the disciple to be like the teacher, and the slave like the master. If they have called the master of the house Beelzebul, how much more will they malign those of his household!

[26]"So have no fear of them; for nothing is covered up that will not be uncovered, and nothing secret that will not become known. [27]What I say to you in the dark, tell in the light; and what you hear whispered, proclaim from the housetops. [28]Do not fear those who kill the body but cannot kill the soul; rather fear him who can destroy both soul and body in hell. [29]Are not two sparrows sold for a penny? Yet not one of them will fall to the ground apart from your Father. [30]And even the hairs of your head are all counted. [31]So do not be afraid; you are of more value than many sparrows.

[32]"Everyone therefore who acknowledges me before others, I also will acknowledge before my Father in heaven; [33]but whoever denies me before others, I also will deny before my Father in heaven.

[34]"Do not think that I have come to bring peace to the earth; I have not come to bring peace, but a sword.

[35] For I have come to set a man against his father,
    and a daughter against her mother,
    and a daughter-in-law against her mother-in-law;
[36] and one's foes will be members of one's own household.
[37] Whoever loves father or mother more than me is not worthy of me; and whoever loves son or daughter more than me is not worthy of me; [38]and whoever does not take up the cross and follow me is not worthy of me. [39]Those who find their life will lose it, and those who lose their life for my sake will find it.

Go on a Specific Mission (10:5–10)

Jesus selected twelve apostles (see 10:1–4). The number "twelve" was significant to Israelites, a number connected usually to the people of God. For example, the twelve tribes of Israel were those who had been called to faithful relationship to God. They were to be a people through whom God would establish relationship with the other peoples of the world. So, the number twelve symbolized God's people.

> *Jesus' ministry made people whole as he delivered them from evil, disease, and sickness.*

Jesus deliberately chose twelve. By this means he symbolized that he was reconstituting Israel. "These twelve" (10:5), therefore, go on mission to Israel, not to the Gentiles or Samaritans. The mission is to gather Israel into the reign of Christ. Although the mission here was to the "lost sheep of the house of Israel" (10:6), Gentiles were not to be excluded on other missions. In fact, the Gospel of Matthew ends with Jesus' charge to his disciples to "go therefore and make disciples of all nations" (28:19). The mission at this point was specific, but it was only part of a total mission to the world.

As these apostles went, they went to a people of very limited resources, of poverty in many cases. Going with no money and limited clothing (10:9–10) helped them identify with the people who needed to hear and respond to the preaching of the kingdom of God. The apostles' focus was not to be on things or acquiring things. This mission was intense. They were not to be encumbered by attention to money or clothes.

Too, they were to trust that their needs would be met. As they preached the kingdom or rule of God in Jesus Christ, resources of the kingdom were sufficient to meet the needs of the king's servants. Going with little to meet their needs kept them open to dependence on the rule of God in their lives.

> *The church participates in Jesus' ministry today as it goes to the harvest under the call of Christ.*

They had "received without payment" (10:8b), and they were to give without payment. The compassion and authority of Jesus by which they were to go on mission were gifts from Jesus. They were to share the gifts from Jesus freely with everyone.

They were, however, to be supported. Jesus said that "laborers deserve their food" (10:10), which meant that those who received the apostles' mission and ministry should give in return. The motivation for the giving lay in the apostles' needs and especially in the value of the message and the mission. By supporting the mission by which the message came, the recipients of the apostles' ministry made it possible for the mission to continue and go on to others.

Overall, by not demanding payment, the apostles on mission distinguished themselves from traveling philosophers and teachers who sometimes took advantage of peoples' generosity in order to gain financial advantage for themselves. One can only think at this juncture of the lavish way in which some present day "proclaimers" of the gospel live and support themselves.

Also, Jesus and the charge he gave to the apostles contrast with what is called the "health and wealth" gospel of today. The "health and wealth" gospel basically says, *Follow Jesus and you will be healthy and wealthy. Good fortune and personal advantage will be yours.* This kind of message can only be described as a perversion of the gospel.

While blessings abound in the service of Christ, they come from a motivation of giving as Jesus gave, not from a desire for personal advantage. Especially is the lack of seeking possible advantage evident in light of this lesson's next section.

Texas Baptists on Mission

N.T. Wright in a penetrating historical analysis of first-century Christianity remarks that "the single most striking thing about early Christianity is its speed of growth. In AD 25 there is no such thing as Christianity. . . . By AD 125 the Roman emperor has established an official policy in relation to the punishment of Christians." In giving the reason for this spread, Wright says that these early Christians believed that what they "had found to be true was true for the whole world. The impetus to mission sprang from the very heart of early Christian conviction."[1]

When we consider how few resources those early Christians had, the march of Christianity is more remarkable. They at first had no buildings except their homes; they had very little money; and they had no status, position of power, or significant recognition in the political and religious structures of that day. We have something for Texas and for the whole world—the gospel. The very nature of the gospel calls us to be on mission.

The Cost of Going (10:24–33)

Some people rejected the kingdom of God, that is, the rule of God in Jesus Christ, which came in the words and actions of Christ. They called Jesus by the stinging name of "Beelzebul" (10:25). Beelzebul was the prince of demons, ruling over and giving directions to the demons of his domain. The disciples, because they carried the same message of Jesus, could expect name-calling themselves. Demonizing someone is one of the most destructive ways to destroy credibility or value. Racism is a form of demonizing. Christians have been, and sometimes still are, discredited by being called crazy, radical, ignorant, or some other negative appellation. They have been treated harshly, verbally and physically, and they have experienced the name-calling rejection Jesus received.

In the face of such treatment, Jesus admonished his disciples to have "no fear" (10:26). The truth and the right will be known and eventually authenticated. Resistance and limited criticism, as harsh as it might seem, was not to deter them. They were to declare the message "from the house-tops" (10:27), therefore, whatever might come. The gospel uncovers what is wrong and emphasizes the right boldly and openly. The evil would be shown, then or later, for what it was. Jesus assured his disciples of the vindication of themselves and their message.

Wholeness in peoples' lives results from Christ's ministry in and through his disciples, the church.

Their fearlessness was to be based on the sovereignty of God over all. While evil could hurt and even kill, God has the power to give life that is eternal (10:28). To turn away from God is to turn to destruction, for then one embraces "hell," which is ongoing destruction. The disciple is to "fear"—revere in thought and action—the one who has the authority and the power to decide eternal destinies (10:28). God will give the victory to his cause.

"Body and soul" (10:28) does not mean here that a person is made up of two compartments, a body and a soul. From the biblical point of view, a person is a soul. The totality of the person is soul. Jesus referred to body and soul to contrast the temporary with the eternal. Investing life in the eternal is much the superior choice.

At the same time, the knowledge of and care for those on mission is specific and detailed (10:29–33). The Father in heaven, the sovereign God and Creator of all things, notices the sparrow that falls to the ground. To notice is to care, and so the point is that God cares for sparrows. Think, then, how much more valuable a person is than the sparrows. Even the "hairs of your head are all counted" (10:30). The Father knows us and values us.

The Priority of Christ (10:34–39)

The kingly and benevolent rule of God in Christ Jesus takes priority over every other element of life. To ask people to reorder priorities so as to put Christ as Lord of life does not always receive favorable response. Jesus prepared his disciples to expect rejection even from some people very close to them, perhaps from members of their immediate family. Therefore, he warned of the "sword" (10:34).

The sword in this text symbolizes separation, not physical violence. The sword cuts one thing away from another, destroying the unity of the original. What is it that makes such a separation in some families as Jesus described? It is the decision to come under the reign of Christ. That decision is the sword. "Set . . . against" father, mother, etc., meant decisions and directions in life made against the wishes even of family, not some hostile conflict (10:35). While Jesus experienced many people, he never rejected anyone who came to him. Even his confrontational words with some people were meant to overcome and break down barriers that stood between him and them. His invitation to share relationship with him was open to everyone.

Do not put self down. Rather, put selfishness down, and give the self you value to Christ, who values you.

At first glance, someone might consider as selfish on Christ's part the demand that he be first. Remember, however, that God comes in Christ to save and deliver. Does Christ need to be loved for his own sake? No, God in Christ has no needs. But we need to be loved by God, and when we put Christ first, we open our lives and all our relationships to God's love. This relationship enhances, makes richer or fuller, and indeed makes possible, healthy and meaningful family relationships.

Therefore, one is to "take up the cross and follow" (10:38). Death was the meaning of the cross in New Testament times, because the cross meant death to the one affixed there. The cross image is a means of emphasizing the importance of Christ's priority in our lives. Every self-serving, self-glorifying matter or thing that could occupy the place of priority is crucified to us by making Christ first.

Note that taking up the cross is not a losing of life but a finding of life (10:39). In contrast, those who grasp life self-centeredly never really live.

Jesus is not calling us to put him first in order to put ourselves down as being unworthy people. Indeed, the very fact that Christ gave himself for us, even when we were against him (Romans 5:8), shows how much he values us. Do not put self down. Rather, put selfishness down, and give the self you value to Christ, who values you.

While blessings abound in the service of Christ, they come from a motivation of giving as Jesus gave, not from a desire for personal advantage.

QUESTIONS

1. What is your missionary work in and through the church?

2. Do you believe resources for your mission are available?

3. Who or what is first priority in your life?

4. Are you "losing life" or "saving life" as Jesus described saving and losing life (Matt. 10:39)?

NOTES

1. N. T. Wright, *The New Testament and the People of God*, I (Minneapolis: Fortress Press, 1992), 359–360.

Focal Text

Matthew
11:2–6,16–30;
12:15–21

Background

Matthew 11:2—12:21

Main Focus

Jesus, who is God's Son
and the Servant
Messiah, invites people
to come to him in
humble trust.

Study Aim

To clarify who Jesus is
and respond to him in
humble trust

Question to Explore

What is revolutionary about the invitation of
Christ?

Texas Priorities Emphasized

- Share the gospel of Jesus Christ with the
people of Texas, the nation, and the world
- Minister to human needs in the name of
Jesus Christ
- Equip people for ministry in the church
and in the world

LESSON SIX

Invited to Come

Quick Read

Jesus issues a warm, open invitation for all to
come to him for salvation and fulfillment in life.

Don was very ill but getting better. Throughout his ordeal he received the ministry of the church. The church cared in the name of Christ in both word and deed. One day at his home, as we sat talking, Don said in answer to a question, "Yes, that is what I want to do. I want to accept Christ and be baptized." He responded to the loving invitation of Christ.

Consider how invitation may be viewed in Don's situation. First, Don's need was an invitation to the church to minister. Jesus teaches the church to see people's needs and move to meet them, both their immediate needs and the need for forgiveness of sin and the gift of eternal life. Second, the church's ministry was an invitation to Don. The ministry was a witness to the care and acceptance of Christ and to the salvation offered in Christ. Third, in and through all of this was the ministry of the presence of Christ, inviting Don into eternal relationship to him.

The focal texts today show Jesus in a ministry of invitation to Israel. The long-awaited expectation for a deliverer was fulfilled in Jesus Christ. Matthew pictures Jesus setting out to gather Israel, with all their various problems, to himself, so that they might be delivered into the life God wanted for them. He invited everyone, especially those among the powerless and the unwanted.

John the Baptist and the Invitation of Christ (11:2–6)

In Matthew's Gospel, John burst on Israel's scene (3:1–6) with surprising appearance and impact. He called people to repentance. They responded, submitting to John's baptism as a sign of their repentance. They, John told them, were preparing for the coming of the Messiah, the promised deliverer of Israel. Expectations were high, especially among John the Baptist and his disciples.

Jesus surprised many with his approach. Again, especially surprised was John the Baptist. Jesus arrived on the scene and began a self-giving ministry to the powerless, the outsiders, the untouchables, and the unwanted. A great ministry indeed, but where was the condemnation of Roman oppression? Where was the judgment on the corrupt religious practices? Where were the calls to mobilize the people for resistance? And where were the spectacular displays of power that would cause all the oppressive political and religious powers to hide from the Messiah? So John the Baptist wondered what Jesus was doing. Was there another, a second Messiah, to come and accomplish these things? John sent his associates to ask.

Matthew 11:2–6,16–30

²When John heard in prison what the Messiah was doing, he sent word by his disciples ³and said to him, "Are you the one who is to come, or are we to wait for another?" ⁴Jesus answered them, "Go and tell John what you hear and see: ⁵the blind receive their sight, the lame walk, the lepers are cleansed, the deaf hear, the dead are raised, and the poor have good news brought to them. ⁶And blessed is anyone who takes no offense at me."

· ·

¹⁶"But to what will I compare this generation? It is like children sitting in the marketplaces and calling to one another,

¹⁷ 'We played the flute for you, and you did not dance;
    we wailed, and you did not mourn.'

¹⁸For John came neither eating nor drinking, and they say, 'He has a demon'; ¹⁹the Son of Man came eating and drinking, and they say, 'Look, a glutton and a drunkard, a friend of tax collectors and sinners!' Yet wisdom is vindicated by her deeds."

²⁰Then he began to reproach the cities in which most of his deeds of power had been done, because they did not repent. ²¹"Woe to you, Chorazin! Woe to you, Bethsaida! For if the deeds of power done in you had been done in Tyre and Sidon, they would have repented long ago in sackcloth and ashes. ²²But I tell you, on the day of judgment it will be more tolerable for Tyre and Sidon than for you. ²³And you, Capernaum,

will you be exalted to heaven?

No, you will be brought down to Hades.

For if the deeds of power done in you had been done in Sodom, it would have remained until this day. ²⁴But I tell you that on the day of judgment it will be more tolerable for the land of Sodom than for you."

²⁵At that time Jesus said, "I thank you, Father, Lord of heaven and earth, because you have hidden these things from the wise and the intelligent and have revealed them to infants; ²⁶yes, Father, for such was your gracious will. ²⁷All things have been handed over to me by my Father; and no one knows the Son except the Father, and no one knows the Father except the Son and anyone to whom the Son chooses to reveal him.

²⁸"Come to me, all you that are weary and are carrying heavy burdens, and I will give you rest. ²⁹Take my yoke upon you, and learn from me; for I am gentle and humble in heart, and you will find rest for your souls. ³⁰For my yoke is easy, and my burden is light."

Matthew 12:15–21

15When Jesus became aware of this, he departed. Many crowds followed him, and he cured all of them, 16and he ordered them not to make him known. 17This was to fulfill what had been spoken through the prophet Isaiah:

18 "Here is my servant, whom I have chosen,
my beloved, with whom my soul is well pleased.
I will put my Spirit upon him,
and he will proclaim justice to the Gentiles.
19 He will not wrangle or cry aloud,
nor will anyone hear his voice in the streets.
20 He will not break a bruised reed
or quench a smoldering wick
until he brings justice to victory.
21 And in his name the Gentiles will hope."

Jesus responded with what we might consider an unusual answer. He told John's associates to tell John what they heard and saw. What did they "hear and see" (11:4)? They saw the blind, the lame, the lepers, the deaf, the dead, and the poor as a focus of the delivering work of Jesus. Notice again that Jesus did not focus on the powerful and notable people (although some of those did respond). Consider this: If you wanted to cause a comprehensive social, political, and economic turnaround, would you start your movement among the weak instead of the powerful?

To allow one's wisdom and intelligence to be greater than the revelation of God in Jesus Christ is to close oneself off from the greatest wisdom and intelligence of all, the "hidden" things (11:25) of God.

Of course, the ministry of Jesus did show his power over evil and death, over hurt, pain, and oppression of all kinds. These are the real hostage holders of people. Jesus' expression of power over these oppressors was actually a sign that he indeed was the long awaited Messiah. Surely the people and John could see that.

John the Baptist, as great and significant as he was as a prophet, could not perceive things to the depth and breadth of Jesus. He could not know the real nature of God's kingdom until it was made known in Jesus Christ. We should not be surprised that John misunderstood Jesus. Human beings do not easily understand the ways of God. Even those closest to Jesus, his apostles, often misunderstood what he was about.

How well do we see and understand? We sometimes mistakenly think that in order to change the world we ought to appropriate all the political and economic power we can muster or take. The church faces the temptation to think like John rather than like Christ. At times in history the church has aligned itself with the power of governments and cultures that were the instruments for the oppression of people. When the church does so, it loses its identity and its witness to Christ.

> *John the Baptist, as great and significant as he was as a prophet, could not perceive things to the depth and breadth of Jesus.*

The church, however, should challenge the political, social, and economic structures of today. In issuing Christ's invitation to come to the liberation and liberty that he offers, the church is to work against those structures that enslave people. The church, though, is to do this by the power of Christ, not by grasping the powers of the state and bringing those under the church's authority. Such work is part of what makes the invitation of Christ authentic. When we oppose the unrighteousness that takes people captive, we participate with Christ in changing the world to his way.

Jesus' encounter with John's disciples ended with a beatitude, a statement about a condition or attitude that one should have: "And blessed is anyone who takes no offense at me'" (11:16). Knowing Jesus brings us to Jesus. As he appeared too radical to his critics then, he appears radical in the present as well. To be offended by him is to reject him as the person he is, hoping that he might become more in the image we would make him. To be offended by him is to reject his invitation to discipleship, the way of life to which he calls us.

> *Jesus is the key to our understanding of the rest of God's revelation.*

Jesus' ministry enables the church to see clearly the invitation that it is to issue and that it is to follow. The church is to seek out human needs and preach and live Christ there. Also, the church is to realize always that Jesus is there before us, inviting us to go further into our discipleship than we have gone before. We cannot, therefore, consider ourselves to have arrived when we have become the disciples of Christ. We are invited to grow and change as surely as was John the Baptizer.

Failure to Respond to the Invitation (11:16–24)

Jesus confronted the unwillingness of people to hear and respond to the kingdom rule of God breaking into their lives. He depicted this unwillingness in terms of a brief parable. Children play games of "wedding" and "funeral" in the marketplace. When either game is in progress, some children sit on the side and refuse to participate. The picture of children sulking on the sidelines away from the action because they do not get their way is an uncomfortable likeness of some of us at times.

Jesus' ministry enables the church to see clearly the invitation that it is to issue and that it is to follow.

The "generation" (11:16) of Jesus wanted its way and not God's way. John the Baptist came calling people to repentance, and some people branded him as mad, in effect. They refused to ready themselves for the coming of the Messiah. To them, John was not the messenger, and neither did he have the message they wanted to hear. They found him strange, unbending. Like children, they pouted and refused to participate, because John did not bring them a game they wanted to play.

The same was true of Jesus. His personality and practice were so different from John's, but he was not what they wanted either. Like children,

Rest and Yoke

The idea of "rest" was important in Israel's thinking. The Sabbath, the day of rest, pointed backwards to the Creator, who rested on the seventh day (Genesis 2:2–3) and who established a covenant with them. The Sabbath was a sign of the covenant relationship Israel had.

Israel also developed the idea of rest in other ways. For example, rest means cessation from wanderings and from the threats of enemies (Deuteronomy 12:9–10). Rest also means the presence of contentment and security (Isaiah 30:15: Psalm 37:7). By offering rest, Jesus offered release from that which burdens one down (Matt. 11:28).

Jesus invited his hearers to take his yoke upon them. His yoke was "easy" and "light" (11:30). The yoke, a bar put across animals' necks and held in place by a rope under the neck, united two animals in pulling a burden. A yoke figuratively could mean a burden or hardship (1 Kings 12:4; Jeremiah 27:8). That Jesus' yoke was not burdensome meant that becoming his disciple was a way of life that benefited the disciple.

they pouted, sat on the sidelines, and refused to join in. Jesus came with the joyous good news of deliverance and blessings. He invited people to celebrate with him, to share the joy because the rule of God had arrived in a special way in Jesus. Again, they refused to hear and respond.

In Matthew 11:20–24, Jesus took some cities of Galilee to task— Chorazin, Bethsaida, and even Capernaum. Capernaum served as something of his headquarters town while he engaged in his mission to Galilee. No indication exists that these Galilean cities committed the atrocities of Tyre, Sidon, or Sodom, Old Testament cities of evil. Why did Jesus condemn them as he did? By using these exaggerated statements to drive home a point, Jesus could shock the people into seeing the seriousness of rejecting God's work. "Deeds of power" (11:23) had been done in them, deeds of power to be expected when the Messiah came. Yet these cities refused to see and hear and respond.

When we oppose the unrighteousness that takes people captive, we participate with Christ in changing the world to his way.

Jesus also brought into contrast the "wise and intelligent" and "infants" (11:25–26) in order to show the stubborn resistance to his kingdom. The normal order of things is for the wise and intelligent to teach and lead the infants. But things were out of order here. It was not the wise and intelligent but the "infants" who led the way. Childlike faith (not childish) often sees the most and responds the best because preconceived ideas and previous commitments do not get in the way. What was plain enough for infants to comprehend, the adults and intelligent—those with experience and knowledge—simply refused to understand. To allow one's wisdom and intelligence to be greater than the revelation of God in Jesus Christ is to close oneself off from the greatest wisdom and intelligence of all, the "hidden" things (11:25) of God.

Jesus is the source of knowledge about God. Jesus is who God is to us, what God is like, and how God feels about us. Moses and the Law were important. However, those who respond in faith to Jesus have more than the Law God gave; they have God. Jesus takes priority over every other means of knowing God, for "no one knows the Father except the Son" (11:27). Jesus is the key to our understanding the rest of God's revelation. By seeing, hearing, and responding to Jesus, we are seeing, hearing, and responding to God. And, of course, he invites us to do so.

The Great Invitation (11:28–30)

Following the words of confrontation and condemnation, Jesus issued the most compassionate invitation found anywhere (11:28–30). He invited the weary burden-bearers to rest. He invited people to take his yoke upon them.

The rest and yoke of which Jesus spoke had to do with the way of following and serving God in contrast to other "yokes" and "rests" offered. In particular, the yoke of the Law as applied by the scribes and Pharisees was particularly burdensome. To yoke oneself to their approach to the Law was not the way of rest.

Jesus is the direction for anyone to go who needs rest.

The people whom Jesus addressed knew what heavy burdens were. Taxation was high, unemployment was high, and a great gap existed between the few rich and the multitudes of the poor. There was practically no middle class. The social situation was oppressive, a very ill fitting yoke to live under. Too, Israel knew the yoke of Rome, one that they dearly wanted to throw off. These were heavy yokes indeed.

"Come to me," the invitation of Jesus, was the direction and place to go to find "rest" (11:28). Jesus is the direction for anyone to go who needs rest. This is a specific direction to a specific person; nothing mysterious or confusing exists about the direction for rest. "Come to me" is still Jesus' invitation to all of us.

Invitation to Inclusion (12:15–21)

Jesus challenged the social and political structures around him. Those for whom the political and economic structures offered privilege, power, and

Case Study

A family moves into the neighborhood of a church. The family struggles to make ends meet. Their use of the English language is very limited. Three small children are in the family, ages one year, three-and-one-half years, and six years. What is the church to do? What specifically does the gospel have for this family? How is it best to communicate the gospel to them?

advantage gathered themselves against him. Also, some religious leaders (see 12:14) opposed him. They saw him as a threat to religious purity, purity that was necessary in their view if Israel was to receive the blessing and favor of God. Jesus' inclusiveness in large measure stirred their opposition against him. His invitation for all to come and become part of the redeemed Israel of God did not distinguish properly to their satisfaction between the pure and the impure. But Matthew (12:18–21) points out, in a rendition from Isaiah 42:1–4, that Jesus' action reflected the action of God's expected servant, who would be inclusive. Jesus is that Servant-Messiah of their expectation, inviting all to participate in his kingdom.

Matthew's Gospel makes apparent, as do other New Testament writings, that Jesus Christ is for everybody.

Therefore God's care for all, his invitation to all equally, finds ultimate expression in Jesus Christ. This is well pleasing to God. Such inclusiveness is good news for the oppressed, for justice is proclaimed (12:18), and justice will be brought "to victory" (12:20). This justice is not only for the oppressed of Israel, but for the Gentiles (12:18). Thus God's justice is all-inclusive.

With Jesus, the Promised Land is neither for a particular people nor a particular land, but for the whole world. Remember that Matthew's Gospel ends with the Great Commission, a commission that sends disciples out to make disciples of all nations (28:19)

Note in 12:20–21 that Jesus' strength comes in compassion, not in violence. "He will not break a bruised reed or quench a smoldering wick" pictures the non-violence and compassion in his movement (12:20). A bruised reed was one just ready to break, and a smoldering wick was one about to extinguish itself. Jesus' movement had such an absence of violence that not even a very weak reed or very tiny wick flame would feel pressure.

The example and message of the Messiah are clear for the church today. We are called to be on mission. Mission beats in the content of the gospels and other writings of the New Testament. Matthew's Gospel makes apparent, as do other New Testament writings, that Jesus Christ is for everybody. Special attention is to be given to the powerless, the disenfranchised, and those who live under injustice. Christ invites us to come, and he includes everyone, even me. It is a warm, open invitation to those who are weary and burdened and need rest, even to me and to you.

QUESTIONS

1. What are some examples of unjust structures in our society today?

2. What should the church do about them?

3. Is it possible to be selective in how we picture Jesus so that he will not make us too uncomfortable?

4. How open are we to others in issuing the invitation of Jesus?

5. What does the invitation to take Jesus' yoke mean to you?

Time to Decide

Unit Four, Time to Decide, consists of two lessons from Matthew 13—16. The first lesson treats the third major discourse of Jesus in Matthew's Gospel. In this discourse Jesus used parables to convey his message about the kingdom of heaven. The background Scripture for this lesson is Matthew 13:1–52. In the first year of the release of this issue of *Bible Study for Texas*, the study of this lesson may occur on Easter. Therefore, a passage on the resurrection of Jesus, Matthew 28:1–6, also is included in this study of "What Faith Is Worth," reminding us of the importance of Jesus' resurrection to our faith.

The background passage for the second lesson is Matthew 13:53—16:28. This lesson considers Jesus' question to Peter about Jesus' identity, Peter's response to the question, and Jesus' teaching that followed about the nature of discipleship.[1]

UNIT 4: TIME TO DECIDE

Lesson 7 What Faith Is Worth   Matthew 13:24–46; 28:1–6

Lesson 8 What Faith Costs   Matthew 16:13–26

NOTES

1. Unless otherwise indicated, all Scripture quotes in Unit 4, Lessons 7–8, are from the New Revised Standard Version.

Focal Text
Matthew 13:24–46;
28:1–6

Background
Matthew 13:1–52;
28:1–6

Main Focus
In spite of all appearances, the ultimate victory of Jesus' way is certain, making commitment to him worth all a person has.

Study Aim
To identify implications of the ultimate victory of Jesus' way

Question to Explore
Why bother with serving God?

Texas Priorities Emphasized
- Share the gospel of Jesus Christ with the people of Texas, the nation, and the world
- Equip people for ministry in the church and in the world

LESSON SEVEN

What Faith Is Worth

Quick Read
To become a part of the kingdom of God in Jesus Christ is worth all a person has.

Experiences and events such as birth, death, marriage, tragedy, and achievements cast shadows and light over life. Every life is a mixture of shadows and light. But is there a light so strong and powerful that it illumines the shadows and brings under its brightness all the experiences we have? For Christians there is—the resurrection of Jesus Christ.

The resurrection of Jesus Christ is the central event of Christianity. It is the reality of the defeat of sin and evil, which brings the dark shadows into life. The lesson ends with the passage about the resurrection (28:1–6), appropriate not only for the Easter season but also for all the years of our life.

But first, we deal with the third of five discourses (a discourse is a lengthy statement about a subject or subjects) in the Gospel of Matthew. This discourse views the kingdom, the rule of God in Christ, primarily in the form of parables. The first readers of the parables of the Gospel of Matthew lived on this side of the resurrection, as we do, and saw the parables in that light. The parables told them much about the kingdom of heaven.

A parable may be a short saying as a simile or metaphor, or it may be a longer saying in the form of a story. A parable is not an allegory. In an allegory, each part of a story has meaning within itself either loosely connected or unconnected to the total meaning of the story. A parable, while it may have allegorical characteristics, has an overall thrust to which the parts of the story adhere closely. Usually, the major thrust of a parable is found in its conclusion. Too, a parable has openness to it as to its meaning. One person may see aspects or applications of it that another does not see.

One caution is appropriate here, however. We should remember that when Jesus spoke his parables he did so in a given situation to a given people for a particular purpose. While we cannot put ourselves back into that situation entirely, keeping that in mind may guard us from the wild and fanciful interpretations that sometimes occur. If in our interpretation of a parable the meaning does not somehow relate to the situation of Jesus' hearers, then we would do well to reconsider our interpretation.

The kingdom of God, or kingdom of heaven (see article), was central in Jesus' preaching and teaching. One of his favorite ways of speaking about the kingdom was through parables. As a parable begins, we often read, "The kingdom of heaven is like." This phrase occurs over and over again in Matthew 13.

Not only do the parables teach us about the kingdom, but they also help us understand how to respond to the kingdom. For example, what is it worth for us to be in the kingdom? How important is the kingdom? How are we to think about the kingdom? What is the value of faith in the kingdom? Indeed, as this lesson asks, in the light of kingdom parables and the resurrection, what is faith worth?

Matthew 13:24–46

24He put before them another parable: "The kingdom of heaven may be compared to someone who sowed good seed in his field; 25but while everybody was asleep, an enemy came and sowed weeds among the wheat, and then went away. 26So when the plants came up and bore grain, then the weeds appeared as well. 27And the slaves of the householder came and said to him, 'Master, did you not sow good seed in your field? Where, then, did these weeds come from?' 28He answered, 'An enemy has done this.' The slaves said to him, 'Then do you want us to go and gather them?' 29But he replied, 'No; for in gathering the weeds you would uproot the wheat along with them. 30Let both of them grow together until the harvest; and at harvest time I will tell the reapers, Collect the weeds first and bind them in bundles to be burned, but gather the wheat into my barn.'"

31He put before them another parable: "The kingdom of heaven is like a mustard seed that someone took and sowed in his field; 32it is the smallest of all the seeds, but when it has grown it is the greatest of shrubs and becomes a tree, so that the birds of the air come and make nests in its branches."

33He told them another parable: "The kingdom of heaven is like yeast that a woman took and mixed in with three measures of flour until all of it was leavened."

34Jesus told the crowds all these things in parables; without a parable he told them nothing. 35This was to fulfill what had been spoken through the prophet:

"I will open my mouth to speak in parables;
I will proclaim what has been hidden from the foundation of the world."

36Then he left the crowds and went into the house. And his disciples approached him, saying, "Explain to us the parable of the weeds of the field." 37He answered, "The one who sows the good seed is the Son of Man; 38the field is the world, and the good seed are the children of the kingdom; the weeds are the children of the evil one, 39and the enemy who sowed them is the devil; the harvest is the end of the age, and the reapers are angels. 40Just as the weeds are collected and burned up with fire, so will it be at the end of the age. [41]The Son of Man will send his angels, and they will collect out of his kingdom all causes of sin and all evildoers, [42]and they will throw them into the furnace of fire, where there will be weeping and gnashing of teeth. [43]Then the righteous will shine like the sun in the kingdom of their Father. Let anyone with ears listen!

[44]"The kingdom of heaven is like treasure hidden in a field, which someone found and hid; then in his joy he goes and sells all that he has and buys that field.

[45]"Again, the kingdom of heaven is like a merchant in search of fine pearls; [46]on finding one pearl of great value, he went and sold all that he had and bought it.

Matthew 28:1-6

[1]After the sabbath, as the first day of the week was dawning, Mary Magdalene and the other Mary went to see the tomb. [2]And suddenly there was a great earthquake; for an angel of the Lord, descending from heaven, came and rolled back the stone and sat on it. [3]His appearance was like lightning, and his clothing white as snow. [4]For fear of him the guards shook and became like dead men. [5]But the angel said to the women, "Do not be afraid; I know that you are looking for Jesus who was crucified. [6]He is not here; for he has been raised, as he said. Come, see the place where he lay."

The Parable of the Weeds and the Wheat (13:24–30,36–43)

As people tried to understand the kingdom, they wondered, if Jesus is the king from God bringing the kingdom, why is evil not rooted out from Israel? Jesus answered the question with a parable. The interpretation of the parable (13:36–43) shows the sower of the good seed as Jesus, the sower of the weeds as the devil, the field as the world, the wheat as the children of the kingdom, and the weeds as the children of the evil one. The parable ends with the description of the separation of the harvest into their respective destinies.

The resurrection is the confirmation and affirmation of all that Jesus was and did.

Hence, in answer to the question as to why Jesus, if he were king, was not destroying evil like weeds gathered and burned, Jesus said that the time for sowing is now and the time for separation is later. If separation were made now, the good would be uprooted with the bad (13:29). No one would want that. Besides, the critics of Jesus might have been surprised at who the children of the evil one really were. Too, Jesus wanted his sowing to spread the good.

People have the choice to respond to the invitation of Jesus to come into his kingdom and become kingdom children. He is a penetrating influence in humanity. Jesus in and through his church and in the work of the Holy Spirit sows the good kingdom rule among us. Unfortunately, another sower is also at work among us, the evil one. People can make the choice to become children of the evil one as well.

> *What could be more valuable to us than placing faith in Christ, accepting him as Messiah, and thus accepting his rule in our lives?*

Evil is present among us. Even a person who does not believe in God will readily admit that evil is present. We lock our doors, we make laws to restrain the evil, we hire police, and our televisions and computers bring us images of hurt and pain from all over the world. The list of the inhumane acts and attitudes in this field, the world, would be endless. The parable emphasizes, along with its major thrust of picturing what Jesus was doing in his kingdom work, that we are confronted with decision as to our destiny.

Being in the rule of God as known in Jesus Christ is the only good destiny available, for that is where we relate to God. Without God's offer of his rule to us, the only destiny open to us is that of lostness, of destruction. Without God there is no life. God has always entered human existence to offer freely relationship with him. Jesus is the special coming of God into history to offer that relationship freely to us. The parable of the weeds and the wheat stresses how important it is to decide for him.

> *Even when the kingdom cannot be seen, its strength is greater than any other strength, because it is the rule of God.*

What could be more valuable to us than placing faith in Christ, accepting him as Messiah, and thus accepting his rule in our lives? The sowing is going on even now, and the urgency of witness and decision is upon us.

Growth of the Kingdom (13:31–35)

The parables of the mustard seed (13:31–32) and the yeast (13:33) tell of the growth of the kingdom. They are contrast parables, in which the

Kingdom of God, Kingdom of Heaven

Matthew preferred the phrase, "kingdom of heaven," while Mark and Luke employed the phrase, "kingdom of God." These phrases are interchangeable. Matthew may have preferred "kingdom of heaven" because it was more respectful to his Jewish readers. For them, acting with reverence toward God meant not saying God's name but putting a word in place of the name, a word such as "heaven."

The kingdom of God means the rule of God. God is sovereign, and he rules over all kingdoms. The "kingdom" refers to something God does—God rules—rather than to a geographical or a political entity. Kingdoms of that sort may come under the kingdom, but they are not the kingdom. Therefore, one cannot build the kingdom; one can only participate in the kingdom. God is the one who extends his rule, and we simply participate in and identify with that rule.

No one can control God's rule. So, as God exercises his sovereignty, he will accomplish what he intends. Matthew shows Jesus as the very expression of that rule among humanity.

---

movement is from the smaller to the greater. When someone in the time of Jesus wanted to emphasize that something was really small, they sometimes used a proverb, a saying. *That is as small as a mustard seed*, someone might say. We use descriptions in that way, also, just as when saying of someone, *His head is as hard as a rock*.

People expected that when God's kingdom rule finally came to Israel in a special way, the event would be spectacular. Jesus arrived talking about the kingdom and calling people to him to be in the rule of God. As people watched and listened to Jesus, however, they did not see the bonds of Roman rule falling away. They did not see the people they considered most evil running to the mountains to hide. They did not see the people mobilizing behind Jesus as a mighty political and military force. They saw miracles, but others also claimed to be miracle workers. They expected spectacular signs of deliverance beyond what Jesus did. They only saw Jesus and a few disciples, for the most part going quietly about preaching and teaching and helping the weak, the sick, and the poor. Should Jesus not be meeting with the religious leaders in order to mobilize the forces of right? Should he not call the armies of God together?

> The kingdom is a tiny seed, but nothing can stop its growth, not even all the forces of evil.

Jesus had to explain patiently the nature of the kingdom to them. The kingdom begins small, like a mustard seed—so small in fact, that it may be almost unnoticeable to some, for a mustard seed would really have to be noticed to be seen. But the tiny seed grows into a large tree. The "birds of the air" come to "make nests in its branches" (13:32). The kingdom is like that. It begins small but it grows to great proportions.

Although the coming of Jesus Christ may have had small beginnings, look at what has happened over the centuries.

People are not impressed with the small. We mostly are impressed by the large. We speak of the mega-corporation and the mega-church. We have super bowls and huge machines building huge buildings. We are impressed by the large. While there is nothing inherently wrong with the big, Jesus reminds us not to apply the same standards to the kingdom. Even when the kingdom cannot be seen, its strength is greater than any other strength, because it is the rule of God.

The kingdom is a tiny seed, but nothing can stop its growth, not even all the forces of evil. The growth is process and miracle. Thinking of growth as process involves picturing or analyzing each step until the plant reaches maturity. Comparing the beginning and end—tiny seed, huge plant—presents the miraculous

Faith is indeed worthwhile.

aspect. How is that huge plant folded up into that small seed anyway? The whole event is a miracle from this perspective. The same is true of the yeast. A small bit in the flour leavens the whole "three measures" (13:33). The yeast, a tiny part, works its ways throughout the whole. It has an impact all out of proportion to its size.

Although the coming of Jesus Christ may have had small beginnings, look at what has happened over the centuries. Millions now call Christ their Lord, people from every land and almost every language. Christ has influenced literature, art, science, politics, and economics in much of the world. And, of course, his kingdom rule is not over. We see the tree still growing and the yeast still leavening a larger portion.

In these picture stories, parables, Jesus teased peoples' minds and imaginations into understanding what he was doing among them. The use of parables was a prominent way in which Jesus opened up to people what they were unable to see, what had been "hidden" (13:35) from them.

The Value of the Kingdom (13:44–45)

With the parables of the hidden treasure and the pearl of great value, Jesus again offered clear pictures of the worth of God's rule in one's life. A field worker while about his labor stumbles upon treasure of which the owners of the field knew nothing. Sometimes when invading armies came and people had to flee their homes, they buried their treasure in their fields to keep it safe. Some of those people never returned, thus leaving the treasure forgotten to succeeding owners. The worker in the parable stumbles across such previously unknown treasure. He sells everything he has in order to possess the most valuable treasure of all.

Likewise, the pearl merchant finds a valuable pearl. He sells everything he has in order to possess that pearl. However, he does not stumble upon it. Rather it has been the object of a life-long search for him. When he finally finds the object of his earnest search and secures it, deep satisfaction and great joy fill the emptiness where there was something he wanted but did not have.

Jesus was saying that whether people stumble upon the kingdom or discover it by search, they will give up everything to make it theirs if they really understand its value. Nothing—no possession or relationship—is as valuable as the kingdom of heaven.

The Victory of the Kingdom (28:1–6)

The resurrection is the confirmation and affirmation of all that Jesus was and did. When Mary and Mary Magdalene (28:1) came to the burial site, surely they were thinking that the whole event of Jesus' life was over. They were little prepared for what happened. The angel, the stone rolled away, the empty tomb, and the announcement of the resurrection stunned them.

Case Study

This case study, though difficult, happens often and is so much a part of life. A patient has just been told that he or she has only a certain amount of time to live. The patient tells you about it and asks whether there is any comfort or hope you can give. What would you say?

The stone having been rolled away and the angel being present to make the announcement to the women indicate that the empty tomb and the resurrection were all God's doing. An action of God so striking that nothing else could compare with it had occurred in history. The women had every reason to run in terror. What they experienced did not fit into any of the ordinary experiences of life, and so they had nothing to fall back on by way of explanation to give them comfort.

In this setting, though, the women heard words of calming and comfort. "Do not be afraid" (28:5) was the first word. The second word was, "He is not here; for he has been raised" (28:6). That word turned their thoughts away from themselves to Jesus. The announcement meant that he lived; death did not rule over him.

The empty tomb was there for them to see. The power of God in Jesus Christ over death was confirmed.

All of humanity comes to the point of death, to a tomb in effect. The message, "Do not be afraid," stretches across the centuries and comes to us. Do not be afraid of death. Death is conquered in Christ Jesus. Matthew writes this good news so that people will know that in Christ's reign life over death, eternal life is offered to them. Surely people will want to choose life.

Nothing—no possession or relationship—is as valuable as the kingdom of heaven.

A pastor often goes to gravesides to offer care to grieving family members and friends facing the death and separation of someone they loved. If not for the resurrection of Christ, the preacher would have little to say. Perhaps the minister could say, *This person lived a good life; this person loved family and friends; and we sympathize with the grieving family and friends.* Such comments are good but not helpful enough to bring real comfort and hope. Because of Jesus' resurrection, however, the preacher has something more to say. Indeed, so much can be said because of the resurrection. The pastor can call the people's attention to Christ and say of him, "He is not here; for he has been raised" (28:6).

Jesus' resurrection confirms the message of the parables. Faith is indeed worthwhile.

QUESTIONS

1. How does understanding the nature of the kingdom create security for believers?

2. How would you apply the parable of the mustard seed to yourself?

3. Do you think of the kingdom of God as being as valuable as depicted in the parables of the treasure in the field and the pearl of great price?

4. What does the resurrection mean to you?

Question to Explore

What actions of yours indicate real faith in Christ—and what actions do not?

Background
Matthew 13:53—16:28

Main Focus

Jesus calls people who confess faith in him to follow him no matter the cost.

Texas Priorities Emphasized

- Share the gospel of Jesus Christ with the people of Texas, the nation, and the world
- Equip people for ministry in the church and in the world
- Strengthen existing churches and start new congregations

Study Aim

To evaluate whether I have confessed my faith in Christ so that I am committed to following him no matter the cost

LESSON EIGHT

What Faith Costs

Quick Read

Jesus invites us to give life away as his disciple, by which he leads us into really living.

Anything we consider valuable costs something. Whether in participating in sports, gaining an education, rearing children, or conducting business, the cost to us for that which we consider valuable is considerable.

If life is to be expended, do we not think it best to expend it on something worthwhile and not something trivial? A pastor attempted to help a couple repair their marriage. As he talked to them in their big, beautiful house he decided to speak bluntly to the neglectful husband. His words were, "Don't you think a person is pretty much a fool to spend so much time and energy in building a house and fail to build a home?" This lesson calls us to examine that to which we dedicate our real energies and resources.

The Question (16:13–15)

As the reader considers Matthew's account of Jesus up to chapter 16, Jesus' actions and words show that he is the long-awaited Messiah, the king of Israel, and, indeed, of the world. An example will demonstrate the action of the Messiah by which he should have been recognized. Jesus fed the five thousand, just as the people and Moses were fed in the wilderness by the miracle of the manna (14:13–21; see Numbers 11). As God provided food for the people in spite of Moses' doubt, so Jesus provided food in spite of the disciples' doubt. One of the signs of the Messiah would be that he would bring the manna from heaven, demonstrating that the kingdom, the rule of God, had come upon them.

So Jesus was the Messiah, and his actions and words revealed his identity to those prepared to see and listen. The disciples, therefore, observed first hand the remarkable rule of God exercised in Jesus Christ. Their observations and experiences with Jesus conditioned them to answer the important question Jesus had for them.

Jesus asked, "'Who do people say that the Son of Man is'" (16:13)? Jesus wanted his close associates, the twelve apostles, to first tell him what identity people in general gave to him. The apostles knew. The opinions varied. Some said Jesus was John the Baptist. Matthew 14:2 relates that Herod feared that Jesus was John the Baptist come back to life. Others said Jesus was Elijah, or Jeremiah, or one of the prophets. Was he Elijah, whom some expected to precede the coming of the messianic time? Or, was he a prophet like Jeremiah or one of the others? People had difficulty determining Jesus' identity.

Matthew 16:13–26

¹³Now when Jesus came into the district of Caesarea Philippi, he asked his disciples, "Who do people say that the Son of Man is?" ¹⁴And they said, "Some say John the Baptist, but others Elijah, and still others Jeremiah or one of the prophets." ¹⁵He said to them, "But who do you say that I am?" ¹⁶Simon Peter answered, "You are the Messiah, the Son of the living God." ¹⁷And Jesus answered him, "Blessed are you, Simon son of Jonah! For flesh and blood has not revealed this to you, but my Father in heaven. ¹⁸And I tell you, you are Peter, and on this rock I will build my church, and the gates of Hades will not prevail against it. ¹⁹I will give you the keys of the kingdom of heaven, and whatever you bind on earth will be bound in heaven, and whatever you loose on earth will be loosed in heaven." ²⁰Then he sternly ordered the disciples not to tell anyone that he was the Messiah.

²¹From that time on, Jesus began to show his disciples that he must go to Jerusalem and undergo great suffering at the hands of the elders and chief priests and scribes, and be killed, and on the third day be raised. ²²And Peter took him aside and began to rebuke him, saying, "God forbid it, Lord! This must never happen to you." ²³But he turned and said to Peter, "Get behind me, Satan! You are a stumbling block to me; for you are setting your mind not on divine things but on human things."

²⁴Then Jesus told his disciples, "If any want to become my followers, let them deny themselves and take up their cross and follow me. ²⁵For those who want to save their life will lose it, and those who lose their life for my sake will find it. ²⁶For what will it profit them if they gain the whole world but forfeit their life? Or what will they give in return for their life?

Jesus asked what others thought in order to ask the next question, a question asked of the twelve: "But who do you say that I am?" (16:15). The disciples walked with Jesus, talked with Jesus, and most importantly, saw Jesus in action. They heard him teach and preach, and they shared his friendship, compassion, and love. Jesus' life before them pointed them toward the fact that the long-awaited kingly rule of God breaking into history had arrived in Jesus Christ. Had his disciples really understood? Did they see?

The Confession (16:16)

Simon Peter answered with what has been called the great confession. "You are the Messiah, the Son of the living God" (16:16). Simon Peter,

91

Son of Man

Jesus frequently referred to himself as "Son of Man." He is the only one in the gospels who calls himself by that title. While "son of man" meant in some cases simply "I," it certainly had more meaning than that when Jesus used that term.

By tracing the term, we see both the suffering and the glory of Jesus. Jesus employed the title in at least three ways of himself: as one of authority, as one of suffering, and as one who returns. As one of authority, for example, he forgives people of their sins (Matt. 9:6). In the focal text in this lesson, he identifies himself as the Son of Man (16:13). He later tells of his expected suffering (16:21). Mark 8:31; 10:33 and other references tell of the suffering of the Son of Man. Then, too, the Son of Man is one who returns. This understanding is highlighted in Matthew 25:31. While these three uses of the title do not exhaust its meaning, we can understand that Jesus employed the term to help people understand who he was.

often the spokesman for the group, may have spoken for the rest of the twelve on this occasion, not just for himself. The group may have talked together about this matter and reasoned among themselves. They came to agreement about Jesus. Simon expressed their view.

The title for Jesus, "Messiah," comes from the Hebrew word. The title "Christ" comes from the Greek word. The two are the same title in different languages. The title means, "anointed one." In Israel's history, a person such as a king would be anointed for the responsibility to carry out God's will in a given situation at a given time. The Messiah of first-century expectation would come to deliver Israel and rule as God willed. Jesus in his identity as Messiah was the specially anointed king-deliverer for Israel.

The apostles recognized Jesus as that anointed one, the deliverer of Israel. In addition, he is the "Son of the living God" (16:16). In the question Jesus asked and the confession Peter voiced, we have the three major titles of Jesus found in the gospels: Son of Man, Messiah, and Son of God. Of course, "Son of the living God" establishes the apostles' understanding of Jesus' divine identity.

Jesus Builds His Church (16:17–20)

Jesus responded pointedly to the confession. Simon and the others arrived at this confession about Jesus not by their own deduction, as observant as they were, but by the "Father in Heaven" (16: 17). They did not make this up, and Jesus did not force them to this revelation. God took the initiative to bring them to understand the truth about Jesus' identity.

Jesus also spoke to Simon Peter again. Simon was "son of Jonah" (16: 17), but Jesus now called him by the name of "Peter." Peter is the name Jesus gave him. The name Peter is *petros* in the Greek language, which means, "rock." Despite the name, in many ways Simon was not "rock." He was sometimes sand blown about by his own impulsive, passionate nature. Sometimes he acted in the wrong way or spoke wrongly (see 16:23). But while being the son of Jonah (16:17) was good, being made into rock by Jesus was a wonderful direction for his life.

The church is storming the gates of death to rescue people from death to the power of life in Jesus Christ.

Jesus' statement to Simon, *You are rock and on this rock I will build my church*, has at times raised a storm of controversy. The Roman Catholic Church's position has been that Jesus commissioned Simon Peter specifically to become the authority for the church after Jesus. In turn, some designated leader would assume the mantle of authority after Simon Peter, and so on, until the process brings us to the present. The one who is recipient of this authority now thus would be the present pope. This is the doctrine of apostolic succession. The leadership of Simon Peter certainly was important in the early church. Nonetheless, nothing in the rest of the accounts of Simon after the death and resurrection of Jesus indicate that he had this degree of special authority, or that the church considered Simon in this way.

People needed rescuing from the powers that enslaved them, and to do so Jesus engaged the powers of evil and death.

Jesus used different word forms in his statement to Peter. He is Peter, *petros*, and upon this rock, *petra*, Jesus will build his church. In Greek the second word for *rock* is a different word from the first. *Petros* would mean a single rock, which one might pick up from the ground. *Petra* would mean a huge rock, like bedrock, or the outcropping rock from a rock face of a hill or mountain. However, these words might be interchangeable in some cases, and so nothing conclusive can be decided by these word meanings.

The important fact is that the words are different. The demonstrative pronoun "this" in "this rock" also stresses that Jesus meant two different things, one *petros*, the other *petra*. So the second rock, *petra*, refers to something other than Simon Peter.

A traditional way of interpreting this passage is that Jesus builds his church upon the kind of confession made. Anyone who makes a confession like Simon Peter's confession becomes a "rock" in the building of the church. Such a word picture occurs in 1 Peter where the church is referred to as "living stones" built one upon another (1 Peter 2:4–5). As Mathew later asserts, however, Jesus is the rejected stone who has become the "head of the corner" (Matt. 21:42). So the church is given "shape" by him.

The best conclusion seems to be that Simon Peter is something of a representative person for what the church is like. People like Peter who confess as he confesses are the building stones for the church. People like Peter become also those who have authority to carry on the servant-ministry of Jesus.

"Keys" (16:19) are a symbol for the authority that Jesus shares with his church. Peter and people who confess as Simon Peter confessed share that authority (see 18:15, where the whole church has that authority). Peter and the church have the power to "bind" and the power to "loose" (16:19). In exercising this authority, what they bind and loose has been bound and loosed in heaven. In other words, they were to carry out the will of heaven, or God. To bind meant to forbid, and to loose meant to permit. Such authority is not exercised without leadership, and Simon Peter was a significant leader. So were James, Barnabas, Aquila, Priscilla, Lydia, John, Apollos, and others. In reality, it is the church acting together to express this authority that exercises the power of the "keys."

Losing life for Christ's sake, in him and as his disciple, is the only way that life can be found.

The "gates of Hades" cannot stand against the church that Christ builds (16:18). "Hades" is a transliteration of the Greek word. The Greek word *hades* and the Hebrew word *sheol* refer to the same place (see Isaiah 38:10). The place is the place of the dead. As people read "gates" in this passage, they sometimes picture the church in a defensive position with its

Case Study

A man recently won a large sum of money in a lottery drawing. He also was on a list to receive a donor kidney. He said he would gladly give all that money for the kidney. The man believed living was more important than money. What would you say to that man if you could talk to him?

gates closed to evil that keeps trying to crash through the defenses. However, the gates belong to Hades, and it is evil that is on the defensive. The church is storming the gates of death to rescue people from death to the power of life in Jesus Christ.

The Cost to Build the Church (16:21–23)

Jesus' discussion with his disciples about his identity and the building of his church presents a turning point in Matthew's account of Jesus. From this point Jesus headed toward Jerusalem, where he suffered and died on a cross. The cross was the form of capital punishment in that time. People needed rescuing from the powers that enslaved them, and to do so Jesus engaged the powers of evil and death. These powers always find expression in the structures of society, such as in some of the ruling structures found at Jerusalem. Here certain "elders and chief priests and scribes" of the religious establishment (not all were against Jesus) are pointed to as those who would bring Jesus to suffer and die (16:21).

As the way for saving us was costly for Jesus, the way of following Jesus is costly for us.

The necessity for Jesus to suffer and die in order to redeem humanity requires and deserves books of explanations, and many have been written on this subject. Consider this brief statement. Complete innocence, Jesus, met evil in this life and death struggle at the cross so that evil, the powers, had no place to go. Evil can live only off evil. When evil meets the completely innocent one, Jesus Christ, it dies from lack of nourishment. It has no place to which to attach itself. Jesus did not meet hate with hate, hostility with hostility, rejection with rejection, or prejudice with prejudice. Had he done so the powers of evil and the powers of death could have lived beyond him. Rather, he met hate, rejection, and prejudice with acceptance and love. Thus the powers of evil and death died when they met Jesus. But such deliverance was costly. He gave himself. His self-giving on the cross is central to understanding Christ and how much he wants deliverance for humanity. Note

When we come to the cross, and accept God's work there, and when we come to the resurrection, and accept God's work there, the powers of evil and death are finished for us.

also that Jesus practiced what he preached. People bent on doing evil would deliver great suffering for him to bear, but he would forgive them all. He would not return evil for evil (see 5:38–45).

Nonetheless, Jesus had to go to Jerusalem. There he aggressively engaged the evil. Although evil would attempt to hold the completely innocent one in its power, the power of God in Jesus Christ is greater. "On the third day" he would be raised (16:21). When we come to the cross, and accept God's work there, and when we come to the resurrection, and accept God's work there, the powers of evil and death are finished for us.

His self-giving on the cross is central to understanding Christ and how much he wants deliverance for humanity.

Jesus tried to prepare his disciples for his self-giving (16:21), but Simon Peter did not accept his effort. Therefore, Simon Peter rebuked Jesus for announcing his suffering and death (16:22). Peter must have been surprised at Jesus' rebuke of him. He referred to Simon as "Satan" and a "stumbling block." Note that "Satan" contrasts with "Father in heaven" in the previous paragraph (16:17). Simon Peter and the others listened to the wrong one at this point. Jesus' journey to Jerusalem was of divine necessity. Anything standing in the way of this saving path was not on the side of the Father in heaven, but on the side of Satan.

Look at all that we may accomplish or acquire for ourselves, "the whole world" (16:26). Is all that worth our lives?

How much Simon represents human frailty, a rock at one moment and a stumbling block at another. Peter as "stumbling block" contrasts sharply with Peter as "rock", *petros*, as he was named in the previous section (16:18). He and the disciples who agreed with him did not act like building materials. As Simon was representative rock, he became representative stumbling block.

The Cost of Discipleship (16:24–26)

As the way for saving us was costly for Jesus, the way of following Jesus is costly for us. Jesus' way from beginning to now was a way of self-giving for the good of others. One has to give up life for that way and nail self-centeredness and self-promotion to the cross. There they are crucified.

One "loses" life this way. In no way does this mean that self is not valuable, that *you* are not valuable. Rather, self-centeredness is the problem. Losing life for Christ's sake, in him and as his disciple, is the only way that life can be found. This is the way of true self-discovery and self-realization.

On the other hand, people who grasp life to themselves, who live life for themselves while thinking they are saving life, actually lose life (16:25). The option is not there. A person is either in the way of salvation or in the way of lostness. Jesus' invitation to this costly discipleship is not a matter of being one among several choices, it is actually the only choice to keep from losing life.

What do we really value? Look at all that we may accomplish or acquire for ourselves, "the whole world" (16:26). Is all that worth our lives?

QUESTIONS

1. If you listed that which is most valuable to you, what would be first on the list?

2. Is a list really possible? Should it be more of a community of valuables—all that we have and are, taken together—coming under the Lordship of Christ?

3. How does your faith relate to situations that tend to intimidate you?

Pointed Questions and Challenging Answers

This unit deals with passages from Matthew 17—25 and addresses the last two of the five major teaching discourses of Jesus in the Gospel of Matthew. Recall that the first discourse, the Sermon on the Mount in Matthew 5—7, set forth the principles by which Jesus' followers were to live. The second, in Matthew 10, detailed the guidelines the Twelve were to follow in ministry. The third, in Matthew 13, illustrated the nature of the kingdom. With Matthew 18, the fourth discourse, we find Jesus focusing on relationships, dealing especially with forgiveness and family. As the conclusion of his ministry in Galilee neared and his last journey to Jerusalem began, relationships—indeed, confrontations—with his opposition developed. Matthew 21 brings us to the last week of our Lord's earthly ministry, with confrontations that ultimately resulted in his crucifixion.

This unit provides a three-lesson study. Included first is the lesson built on the fourth discourse in Matthew. This lesson emphasizes the radical manner in which commitment to Christ transforms one's relationships. The second lesson in the unit focuses on Matthew 19:1–15, telling of a confrontation between Jesus and the Pharisees concerning marriage and divorce. This passage also touches on singleness and Jesus' attitude toward children. The background for the third lesson in this unit is Matthew 23—25, which contains the fifth discourse of Jesus. After Jesus' scathing rebuke of the Pharisees (Matt. 23), the gospel writer recorded what is often called the Olivet Discourse. This is an important prophetic section, one that contains several passages difficult to interpret. The themes of judgment and preparation dominate chapters 24—25.[1]

MATTHEW: Jesus As the Fulfillment of God's Promises

These three lessons will focus on relationships that are especially important for people today. Concepts that we will examine include:

- the place of forgiveness in Christian living (18:15–35)
- the importance of family as seen in Jesus' teachings on marriage, singleness, and children (19:1–15)
- our responsibility for meeting the needs of those less fortunate than we are (25:31–46)

UNIT 5: POINTED QUESTIONS AND CHALLENGING ANSWERS

NOTES

1. Unless otherwise indicated, all Scripture quotes in Unit 5, Lessons 9–11, are from the New American Standard Bible®.

Question to Explore

What's the name of the person God wants you to forgive today?

Texas Priorities Emphasized

- Share the gospel of Jesus Christ with the people of Texas, the nation, and the world
- Equip people for ministry in the church and in the world
- Develop Christian families
- Strengthen existing churches and start new congregations

LESSON NINE

Will You Forgive?

Quick Read

Forgiveness is at the heart of the Christian life. Because we have been forgiven, we should be willing to forgive those who have wronged us. The principles Jesus taught are to be the guidelines for our extending forgiveness.

The story of Faust is about a man who gambled with his soul, foolishly selling his soul to the Devil for material gain. An artist painted a picture of Faust and Satan playing a game of chess—Faust on one side of the table, Satan on the other. In the painting, the game is almost over, and Faust has only a few pieces left: the king, a knight, and a couple of pawns. The painting has caught the moment when the jubilant Satan has announced a checkmate, and the frightened, despairing Faust has realized he has lost.

Many a chess player had seen the painting and had agreed that Faust's position was hopeless; he had indeed been checkmated. But one day a great master of the game stood gazing at the picture, fascinated by the look of tragic despair on the face of Faust. Then his gaze moved to the pieces on the board. While others in the gallery passed by, in his mind he moved the pieces trying to determine whether Faust could still win. Suddenly he cried out, "It's a lie! The king and the knight have another move!"

Often circumstances seem to say that human experience is hopelessly mired in sin, that our condition is beyond rescue. But Scripture tells us that God has stepped into the picture, offering forgiveness through the death of Jesus. Now, as in the chess game, could we phrase it like this: The King and the Knight have another move!

This lesson deals with forgiveness, a concept at the heart of the Christian message. Jesus had completed an extensive preaching, teaching, and healing ministry in Galilee. At a time of withdrawal with his disciples to the area around Caesarea Philippi, north and east of the Sea of Galilee, Simon Peter had made his great confession (Matt. 16). Then the transfiguration of Jesus had taken place, either on Mt. Hermon or in Galilee on Mt. Tabor (17:1–8). Jesus had clarified that John the Baptist was the fulfillment of the Old Testament prophecy of the return of Elijah (17:9–13). Jesus had healed a child who had what was perhaps an epileptic condition (17:14–21). A second time Jesus had spoken clearly to the Twelve of his approaching death and resurrection (17:22–23; see 16:21). Next Jesus had instructed Peter about paying the temple tax using a miraculous means (17:24–27). Finally, just before the focal text for this study, Jesus had used a child as an object lesson and had spoken of the qualities of a kingdom citizen. This setting became the backdrop for an extensive discourse on forgiveness in 18:15–35.

Matthew 18:15-35

[15]"If your brother sins, go and show him his fault in private; if he listens to you, you have won your brother. [16]"But if he does not listen to you, take one or two more with you, so that BY THE MOUTH OF TWO OR THREE WITNESSES EVERY FACT MAY BE CONFIRMED. [17]"If he refuses to listen to them, tell it to the church; and if he refuses to listen even to the church, let him be to you as a Gentile and a tax collector. [18]"Truly I say to you, whatever you bind on earth shall have been bound in heaven; and whatever you loose on earth shall have been loosed in heaven.

[19]"Again I say to you, that if two of you agree on earth about anything that they may ask, it shall be done for them by My Father who is in heaven. [20]"For where two or three have gathered together in My name, I am there in their midst."

[21]Then Peter came and said to Him, "Lord, how often shall my brother sin against me and I forgive him? Up to seven times?" [22]Jesus said to him, "I do not say to you, up to seven times, but up to seventy times seven.

[23]"For this reason the kingdom of heaven may be compared to a king who wished to settle accounts with his slaves. 24"When he had begun to settle them, one who owed him ten thousand talents was brought to him. [25]"But since he did not have the means to repay, his lord commanded him to be sold, along with his wife and children and all that he had, and repayment to be made. [26]"So the slave fell to the ground and prostrated himself before him, saying, 'Have patience with me and I will repay you everything.' [27]"And the lord of that slave felt compassion and released him and forgave him the debt. [28]"But that slave went out and found one of his fellow slaves who owed him a hundred denarii; and he seized him and began to choke him, saying, 'Pay back what you owe.' [29]"So his fellow slave fell to the ground and began to plead with him, saying, 'Have patience with me and I will repay you.' [30]"But he was unwilling and went and threw him in prison until he should pay back what was owed. [31]"So when his fellow slaves saw what had happened, they were deeply grieved and came and reported to their lord all that had happened. [32]"Then summoning him, his lord said to him, 'You wicked slave, I forgave you all that debt because you pleaded with me. [33]'Should you not also have had mercy on your fellow slave, in the same way that I had mercy on you?' [34]"And his lord, moved with anger, handed him over to the torturers until he should repay all that was owed him. [35]"My heavenly Father will also do the same to you, if each of you does not forgive his brother from your heart."

MATTHEW: Jesus As the Fulfillment of God's Promises

Jesus Gave the Procedure for Forgiveness (18:15–18)

Jesus pictured an individual believer who had become aware of a sin committed by another believer, "your brother" (18:15).[1] A Christian, Jesus said, should not ignore a fault that he sees in a fellow believer but should help him to see his or her sin. The purpose of such a confrontation is to bring the person to repentance.

A word of caution is certainly in order here. Unless the attitude of the concerned Christian is one of love and compassion, such a confrontation can turn to meddling. Paul's admonition in Galatians 6:1 casts light on how such a circumstance is to be approached. Paul wrote, "Brethren, even if anyone is caught in any trespass, you who are spiritual, restore such a one in a spirit of gentleness; each one looking to yourself, so that you too will not be tempted." The Greek verb translated "restore" in Galatians 6:1 is used of setting a broken bone and of mending a torn fishing net. The repair is made so that the person or the net may return to normal service. One's goal in speaking to a fellow Christian about his or her sin should be designed to help the person, not merely to condemn.

Jesus said the approach is first to be made privately, one-on-one. The aim is to solve the problem without involving anyone else. Tragically a personal confrontation is often the *last* step rather than the first, an action taken when nearly everyone knows about the situation! Christians are responsible for one another, but the proper attitude and motive are required. If the offending person responds positively, Jesus said, "You have

"As a Gentile and a Tax Collector"

In Matthew 18:17 Jesus instructed the disciples that they were to treat the unrepentant sinning brother "as a Gentile and a tax collector." Jesus consistently used the term "Gentile" to speak of those who did not know God. The word is translated in the New International Version as "pagan," one who does not know the true God.

The term "tax collector" described those who were tax contractors, members of the local population who bid for the position by guaranteeing the highest amount of money to their superiors. Tax collectors were considered traitors by the Jewish people and consequently were despised and hated. Tax collectors collected money for the hated Roman conquerors. Also, the tax collectors' constant contact with Gentiles rendered them ritually unclean. As well, they were notoriously unscrupulous, growing wealthy at the expense of their own people.

won your brother" (Matt. 18:15). You have rescued a fellow Christian from sin and its consequences, brought the person back to the fellowship of the church, and helped him or her live a fruitful Christian life.

However, not everyone will respond to loving and personal correction. What then?

Second, Jesus said to take one or two other Christians with you and involve them in the discussion (18:16). Such a procedure involves several positive goals. (1) It keeps the situation from becoming a personal matter between only two believers, avoiding the possibility of vindictiveness. (2) It provides witnesses of the attempt to win him from sin. (3) It also provides ample evidence for the church in case the effort does not succeed.

One's goal in speaking to a fellow Christian about his or her sin should be designed to help the person, not merely to condemn.

In giving this instruction in verse 16, Jesus reached back to Deuteronomy 19:15 for this wise principle. Although the circumstances in Deuteronomy related to a judicial trial, the point of the Old Testament reference is the principle that a multiple witness is more convincing.

Years ago in a church in which I served as a pastor, several of the men and I became aware that one of the leaders of the church had been telling an untruth. The result was that the church was being hurt. When this approach commanded by Jesus was followed, the brother faced his wrong, repented openly to the church, and was restored to a place of useful service. The Lord's procedure worked!

But then my fellow Christian wrongs me the third time, and I ask myself the question, How long am I supposed to keep doing this?

Jesus gave his followers a third step (Matt. 18:17). In the event the offending Christian refused to hear this group of two or three, the final recourse was to present the matter to the church, that is, the body of believers. Although Jesus gave no detailed instructions regarding this step, the point is that the grievance was to be made more public. If at this point the offending Christian continued in his or her unrepentant way, the congregation was to dissociate itself from the person. But still, this drastic action was designed to rehabilitate the individual rather than to bring retribution.

Such an example of church discipline is found in 1 Corinthians 5:1–5. Here Paul counseled the church to take public action against a brother involved in an immoral relationship. Paul's wording, "to deliver such a one to Satan for the destruction of his flesh" (1 Cor. 5:5), is understood by many Bible students as meaning to bring about the person's repentance and restoration.

Matthew 18:18 is linked by its wording to Matthew 16:19. The extraordinary authority to interpret the redemptive work of Christ was now given to all the Twelve as it had been given to Peter in chapter 16. The tense of the verb requires that it be translated, "whatever you bind on earth shall have been bound in heaven," with a similar translation of the second half of the verse. Jesus affirmed in advance that the actions and teachings of the Twelve would have spiritual authority. Jesus also here affirmed the authority of the church, his called ones, regarding the withholding or bestowing of forgiveness and fellowship.

Jesus Discussed the Prayer for Forgiveness (18:19–20)

Theses verses have often been taken out of context and consequently terribly misunderstood. That God does not automatically grant every prayer request offered by two or three is obvious. These promises must be linked to the preceding verses. Jesus was here reiterating that actions of Christian discipline in line with his will and purposes have his endorsement. The "two of you" in verse 19 must be linked to the "one or two more with you" in verse 16. The Lord's presence is the divine guidance that empowers his people to act and decide as a Christ-directed church.

> . . . Our gratitude to God for the unconditional forgiveness God has extended to us must be translated into our willingness to forgive others.

These verses affirm that the risen Christ is uniquely present in a Christian gathering as his Spirit indwells believers. Verse 20 particularly assures the Lord's people of his blessing on action properly taken to try to reconcile believers to one another.

Jesus Defined the Proper Extent of Forgiveness (18:21–22)

We are not surprised to hear Simon Peter speak up with a question. He often did exactly that. Someone has suggested that Peter had "foot in mouth" disease; he often opened his mouth and put his foot right into it!

In the general discussion about forgiveness, Peter wanted to know what approach to take to one who sinned against *him*. The rabbis had discussed this subject, deciding that one should forgive another three times. The Babylonian Talmud, an ancient Jewish document, said, "When a man sins against another, they forgive him once, they forgive him a second time, they forgive him a third time, but the fourth time they do not forgive him."

Perhaps that rabbinic teaching was based on the writings of the prophet Amos. In the first two chapters of Amos, the prophet had named enemies of the nation of Israel that surrounded her. He declared that for "three transgressions . . . and for four" (Amos 1:6, for example), God would not revoke his punishment upon those nations. Peter generously proposed that he would forgive a fellow disciple seven times, not just the rabbinic three.

If we are to measure up to Jesus' standard, we are to forgive without keeping track of the number.

Peter's suggestion brings up a very relevant practical question. A fellow Christian sins against me and I stir up enough grace to forgive the person. How very pious that makes me feel! Then the person sins against me again and I reluctantly grant forgiveness a second time. But then my fellow Christian wrongs me the third time, and I ask myself the question, *How long am I supposed to keep doing this?*

Jesus' response to Peter probably stunned him. Jesus said, "I do not say to you, up to seven times, but up to seventy times seven" (18:22). Bible students point out that Jesus' reply is in vivid contrast to Lamech's seventy-sevenfold avenging in Genesis 4:24 as well as to Peter's sevenfold forgiving. The point of our Lord is that legalism and mathematics are not to be considered, but that our forgiving others is to be limitless. Could you keep count of having forgiven someone 490 times? Probably not. If we are to measure up to Jesus' standard, we are to forgive without keeping track of the number. Neither calculator nor computer is required, but only the spirit of Christ.

Jesus Told a Parable Requiring Forgiveness (18:23–35)

Throughout his ministry Jesus often taught by using parables. But what is a parable? Our English word *parable* is the transliteration of a Greek word meaning *to cast along side*. A parable is a short story told by way of analogy

Application Actions

- Reach out to the person in your family from whom you are alienated. Start with a telephone call.
- Reach out to the person in your church family who has hurt you. Pray for tact and guidance.
- Have you been critical of people in places of authority when you should have been praying for them? Ask God's forgiveness, and then intercede on their behalf.

for the purpose of teaching one central truth. A parable is not an allegory, although it may occasionally contain allegorical elements in it. Someone defined a parable as "a handle by which you pick up a truth and carry it home." You likely have heard the short but helpful definition of a parable as "an earthly story with a heavenly meaning."

Jesus illustrated his teachings about forgiveness with the parable of the unmerciful servant. Matthew alone of the four gospel writers recorded it. The central truth of the parable is that God has forgiven us so much; we must therefore be willing to forgive others.

The story is very straightforward. A king wanted to settle his accounts with his slaves. One slave owed the king an enormous debt, a debt of "ten thousand talents" (18:24). Such an amount would startle Jesus' hearers, for a talent was the largest known denomination of money in the ancient world, and ten thousand was the highest number for which the Greeks had a word. The term for *ten thousand* is the one from which we get our word *myriad*. In other words, the sum was a staggering amount. Perhaps we can think of the amount, as a marginal note in the New American Standard Bible® suggests, as being $10,000,000 or more.

> Someone defined a parable as "a handle by which you pick up a truth and carry it home."

Since the slave was unable to pay the debt, the king commanded that he and his entire family be sold. This practice of selling a person and his family when an obligation could not be met was quite common in the ancient world.

When the slave begged for mercy, the king did something astonishing. Rather than give the slave more time to pay the debt, the king forgave the entire debt. Here was amazing grace at work!

Instead of being grateful for his king's act of kindness, the slave demanded payment of a small debt from a fellow slave. Verse 28 tells us that the value of this debt was "one hundred denarii." A denarius was a day's pay for a laborer in that time. What would a denarius be today, given the current minimum wage? Multiply that by one hundred, and the sum still would be very small compared to $10,000,000. Jesus said that the unforgiving slave "seized him and began to choke him" (18:18). Ignoring his fellow slave's pleas for mercy, the unforgiving slave threw the debtor into prison (18:30).

> . . . Jesus expects his followers to have a forgiving spirit.

When the king was told of the matter, he summoned the unmerciful slave, saying, "'Should you not also have had mercy on your fellow slave, in the same way that I had mercy on you?'" (18:33). With this the unforgiving slave was delivered to the "torturers" (18:34).

Have you noticed that unforgiveness so often finds its way into the family circle? Circumstances occur that alienate children from parents and parents from children. Supposed favoritism by a parent toward one child builds walls of unforgiveness. A squabble over the parents' estate causes siblings to develop bitterness that may last for years.

What Jesus Expects

The passages we have examined in this lesson make it quite clear that Jesus expects his followers to have a forgiving spirit. To confront one who has sinned is a delicate and often difficult matter. To forgive is not always easy. To forgive over and over again can be a trying and frustrating experience.

Yet our gratitude to God for the unconditional forgiveness God has extended to us must be translated into our willingness to forgive others. Obedience requires it. Realize that an unforgiving spirit can be like a cancer in the soul, keeping us from that close walk with our Lord that every Christian should desire.

QUESTIONS

1. Is there someone whom you need to forgive today? If so, how will you go about doing this?

2. Are we to forgive people before they ask for forgiveness? Why or why not?

3. How do you see the parable of the unmerciful servant applying to family relationships? to church relationships?

4. Have you heard a person say, "Well, I'll forgive that person, but I won't forget"? Is this following Jesus' principles? Why or why not?

NOTES

1. The phrase translated "against you" (18:15, NIV, NRSV; see also KJV) is missing in several of the better ancient manuscripts, and so it is not included in the New American Standard Bible®.

Main Focus

Jesus calls for husbands and wives to be committed to each other for life, for singleness as well as marriage to be considered acceptable in God's eyes, and for children to be recognized as being of special concern to him.

Study Aim

To summarize Jesus' teachings about marriage, singleness, and the place of children and identify implications for individual Christians and churches

Question to Explore

What does the Christian faith say about marriage, singleness, and the place of children?

Texas Priorities Emphasized

- Share the gospel of Jesus Christ with the people of Texas, the nation, and the world
- Minister to human needs in the name of Jesus Christ
- Equip people for ministry in the church and in the world
- Develop Christian families

LESSON TEN

How Does Faith Affect Family Life?

Quick Read

God's ideal plan for a marriage is one man and one woman for a lifetime. Strengthening families, caring for children, and ministering both to the married and the single must become a top priority.

Statistics prove that Christian marriages are immune from divorce. Right? Wrong! Statistics released by a Christian research group should serve as a wakeup call to Christians and churches.[1] The numbers say that strengthening families and ministering both to the married and the single must become a top priority.

The research group found that among born-again Christians 27% are currently or have previously been divorced, compared to 24% among adults who do not classify themselves as born again. Because of the large number of adults polled in this nationwide survey, the difference is considered statistically significant.

Texas Baptists should be especially interested in and alerted by the regional, ethnic, and denominational differences that the survey revealed. Divorce is much less likely in the northeastern section of our nation than elsewhere. Only 19% of the residents in the Northeast have been divorced, compared to 26% in the West and 27% in both the South and the Midwest. A higher proportion of whites get divorced (27%) than is true among African-Americans (22%) or Hispanics (20%).

Among Christian denominations, Baptists have the highest likelihood of being divorced. Nationally, 29% of all Baptist adults have been divorced. The only Christian group to surpass that level are non-denominational churches (34%). Catholics and Lutherans are the lowest at 21%.

Do these figures say anything to you? They say to me that we must reemphasize the teachings of Jesus regarding divorce and the biblical ideal for marriage. We must as well be more effective in strengthening families. Although the responsibility for the stability of a home depends ultimately on the husband and the wife, our churches have a contribution to make. As well, our churches should reaffirm our responsibility to minister to those who have experienced the tragedy of divorce.

The Confrontation with the Pharisees Concerning Divorce (19:1–9)

This confrontation between Jesus and the Pharisees over the question of divorce took place in the province of Perea, which is the area "beyond the Jordan" (19:1). Very soon Jesus would again be warning the Twelve of his forthcoming death (20:17–19), and he would go through the city of Jericho for the last time (20:29–34), healing two blind men outside the city. Matthew 21—22 tell of the first three days of the last week of the earthy ministry of Jesus, including the Triumphal Entry (21:1–11), the

Matthew 19:1–15

[1]When Jesus had finished these words, He departed from Galilee and came into the region of Judea beyond the Jordan; [2]and large crowds followed Him, and He healed them there.

[3]Some Pharisees came to Jesus, testing Him and asking, "Is it lawful for a man to divorce his wife for any reason at all?" [4]And He answered and said, "Have you not read that He who created them from the beginning MADE THEM MALE AND FEMALE, [5]and said, 'FOR THIS REASON A MAN SHALL LEAVE HIS FATHER AND MOTHER AND BE JOINED TO HIS WIFE, AND THE TWO SHALL BECOME ONE FLESH'? [6]"So they are no longer two, but one flesh. What therefore God has joined together, let no man separate." [7]They said to Him, "Why then did Moses command to GIVE HER A CERTIFICATE OF DIVORCE AND SEND her AWAY?" [8]He said to them, "Because of your hardness of heart Moses permitted you to divorce your wives; but from the beginning it has not been this way. [9]"And I say to you, whoever divorces his wife, except for immorality, and marries another woman commits adultery."

[10]The disciples said to Him, "If the relationship of the man with his wife is like this, it is better not to marry." [11]But He said to them, "Not all men can accept this statement, but only those to whom it has been given. [12]"For there are eunuchs who were born that way from their mother's womb; and there are eunuchs who were made eunuchs by men; and there are also eunuchs who made themselves eunuchs for the sake of the kingdom of heaven. He who is able to accept this, let him accept it."

[13]Then some children were brought to Him so that He might lay His hands on them and pray; and the disciples rebuked them. [14]But Jesus said, "Let the children alone, and do not hinder them from coming to Me; for the kingdom of heaven belongs to such as these." [15]After laying His hands on them, He departed from there.

second cleansing of the temple (21:12–14), the cursing of the fig tree (21:18–22), and several events in what some refer to as "The Day of Controversy" (21:23—22:46).

Matthew's Gospel does not provide extensive details of the Later Judean and the Perean ministries of Jesus. For this information we must turn to John and especially to Luke. In Luke's Gospel we find some ten chapters, 10—19, telling of the events of the last six months of Jesus' ministry. Matthew's account seems to point out that, having left Galilee, Jesus took the route east of the Jordan and passed through Perea. It was in Perea, the long, narrow province east of the Jordan River, that the Pharisees accosted Jesus and asked him the question about divorce.

Built on the Old Testament concept that God hated divorce (Malachi 2:16), Jewish laws regarding marriage and sexual purity set high standards. Unfortunately the practice of the people did not reflect the high aspirations of the laws. The Jewish society of the day of Jesus was a patriarchy; that is, the men were in complete control. A woman was more a thing than a person. She was under the control of her father until she married. In matters concerning divorce, action was initiated almost always by the husband. The wife had only limited protection. If the divorce were for any reason except adultery, the husband had to return the wife's dowry. In Jewish practice, if the husband contracted leprosy, the wife could demand a divorce, but by and large she had few legal rights.

Divorce was a controversial subject then just as it is now. Two opposing schools of thought held to two opposing positions. Both based their teachings on the same Old Testament verse, Deuteronomy 24:1. That verse says, "When a man takes a wife and marries her, and it happens that she finds no favor in his eyes because he has found some indecency in her, and he writes her a certificate of divorce and puts it in her hand and sends her out from his house . . . ." The next verses give the thrust of verse one. The divorced wife, if she married someone else and was divorced the second time, was not permitted to be remarried to the

The Pharisees

The Pharisees were a lay religious body who formed the core of the opposition to the ministry of Jesus. The roots of this group can be traced to the Persian period (539–333 BC) of the interbiblical years, but the Pharisees became a significant force in the Grecian period (333–167 BC). Known as the *hasidim*, "the pious," they defended Judaism and the Mosaic Law against the encroachments of Hellenism. Probably the term "Pharisee" came from the Hebrew word *parash*, meaning "one who is separate."

The Pharisees observed and perpetuated an oral tradition of laws handed down from former teachers and elders of the Hebrew people. Extremely legalistic, the Pharisees advocated a life controlled by literally hundreds of rules and regulations. They believed in a future life of blessedness and the resurrection of the body, but these concepts were quite materialistic in their minds. Emphasizing divine providence, they yet recognized that humans were free moral agents with choices to make. However, not all Pharisees were extreme legalists. Some were genuinely pious—such as Nicodemus and Joseph of Arimathea.

original husband. But verse one contained the critical terms regarding divorce.

The school of Rabbi Shammai focused on the phrase "found some indecency in her." The Hebrew word *indecency* means literally a "matter of nakedness," reflecting some sort of sexual sin, essentially unfaithfulness to the marriage vows. On this basis Shammai taught that adultery was the only acceptable cause for divorce. On the other hand, the followers of Rabbi Hillel pointed to the words, "she finds no favor in his eyes." The followers of Rabbi Hillel concluded that if the wife were "unpleasing" to her husband, that was an adequate reason for him to divorce her. Rabbi Hillel and his followers applied this concept very liberally. If the wife burned the bread or talked negatively about the husband's relatives, or if the husband saw another woman prettier than his wife, his wife became "unpleasing" and could be divorced! Sounds almost like some of the absurd reasons for divorce in our day, doesn't it?

. . . Strengthening families and ministering both to the married and the single must become a top priority.

So the Pharisees, seeking to discredit Jesus, asked him whether it were lawful for a man to divorce his wife "for any reason at all" (Matt. 19:3). Essentially they were asking him whether the school of Hillel were correct. Obviously they were expecting Jesus to take the stricter view of Shammai. Taking Shammai's view would cause Jesus to be unpopular with the people. But Jesus would not be trapped. He mentioned neither Hillel nor Shammai. Going back to God's original design for marriage, Jesus pointed to Genesis 1:27; 2:24. God's plan, Jesus said, was one man for one woman, with the husband's first allegiance to his wife rather than to his parents. Furthermore, since God had made them one, human forces were not to dissolve the union. Divorce was not a part of God's first and ideal plan.

Although the responsibility for the stability of a home depends ultimately on the husband and the wife, our churches have a contribution to make.

The Pharisees objected by asking a second question (Matt. 19:7): *Why then did Moses command a divorce and a written document reflecting the reasons?* In using the word "command" (19:7), they misinterpreted Moses. Jesus responded that Moses did not "command" divorce. Rather Moses *permitted* it, and hardness of heart on the part of the people of Moses' day was the reason for the concession. Jesus then went a step

Application Actions:

- Reach out to someone who is going through the struggle of a divorce and provide a listening ear and caring heart for him or her.
- Take a look at the children's departments and classes of your church. Are there vacancies in teaching or leadership positions in them? Is God leading you to fill one of those vacancies?
- If you have children, affirm their value and your love for them by a thoughtful and special activity with them today.

further than Moses, declaring that the only acceptable reason for divorce is adultery, unfaithfulness to the marriage vows (19:9).

The question always arises as to whether Jesus permitted the innocent party to remarry when a divorce because of adultery has taken place. Jesus gave no direct teaching about this subject in this passage. A strong implication, however, must be considered, and this implication is based on what divorce meant in the Jewish culture of the first century. It seems evident that divorce in the Jewish culture of Jesus' day meant the dissolving of the marriage relationship with the right to remarry. If this is so, then Jesus—by implication—permitted the remarriage of the innocent party.

Since singles are a part of the church family, ministering to the single should be a vital focus for any church.

Another passage we do well to examine briefly in considering this difficult topic of divorce is Paul's discussion in 1 Corinthians 7. We must begin by recognizing that Paul said what he did in chapter seven in the light of these three specific circumstances: (1) that he anticipated the imminent return of Christ in his lifetime; (2) that marriage had fallen to a low state in the pagan world of that day, with immorality the order of the day and sexual purity an unknown virtue; and (3) that Paul himself was single. Paul consequently urged the Christians in Corinth to maintain their present marital status. As well, the statements in this chapter were written to a church where some of the members were glorifying the celibate state. Some were perhaps saying that sexual activity was evil, even within marriage. They thus were contending that a Christian should divorce the husband or wife. In light of these circumstances, Paul addressed several concerns of both married and single individuals.

After urging the unmarried and widows to remain as they were—that is, single—Paul focused on the situation of a believer who was married to an unbeliever (1 Cor. 7:12–17). This could be a perilous situation, especially if the wife were the Christian. Paul urged the believer not to divorce the unbeliever if the unbelieving spouse were willing for the marriage relationship to continue. Verse 15 contains what is often cited as a second Scriptural, acceptable, reason for divorce, with the Matthew 19:9 passage as the first. When an unbelieving spouse deserted a believing husband or wife, Paul declared that the believer was not bound to maintain the marriage. Again the question of remarriage of the divorced believer comes up. Did Paul permit remarriage in this circumstance? It is not clear, for Paul simply did not address this question.

> *"You never know to whom you are speaking when you speak to a child."*

Neither Jesus nor Paul addressed directly other possible reasons for divorce, such as spousal abuse or various other ways in which spouses can make God's ideal for marriage seem—and be—unachievable. As we ponder what to do in hard and heartbreaking circumstances, we do well to recognize that whatever the situation, God still loves us. God never stops wanting to enable us to choose and do what is best in light of the total circumstances and of his plan for our lives.

> *. . . We have the beautiful picture of the Lord placing his hands on these little ones, praying for them and blessing them.*

You may be reading these words and find yourself divorced and single, or divorced and remarried. You may be concerned that circumstances in your divorce, or in your divorce and remarriage, were not pleasing to God. What are you to do? If you have remarried, to dissolve your present marriage would cause more distress and harm, especially in the lives of children in the family. Confession and forgiveness are always available to one of God's children. Remember the words of the Apostle John, who wrote, "If we confess our sins, He is faithful and righteous to forgive us our sins and to cleanse us from all unrighteousness" (1 John 1:9).

The Question of the Twelve (19:10–12)

Jesus' position on divorce, even with the exception clause, was stronger than that of Shammai, and the disciples immediately recognized this. In a parallel passage (Mark 10:10), Mark recorded that the disciples came to Jesus privately, "in the house," asking for clarification. Their statement reflected surprise and consternation. They suggested that if marriage were that binding, perhaps to choose the celibate life would be wiser. The response of Jesus, "Not all men can accept this statement, but only those to whom it has been given" (Matt. 19:10), must be understood accurately. He did not refer to his statements that affirmed the permanence of marriage; this would have contradicted the standard he had just set. It referred rather to the observation of the Twelve suggesting the celibate state was to be preferred.

Three categories of individuals were not to seek marriage, Jesus said. The first group consisted of those with birth defects that made the sexual relationship within marriage impossible. The second group mentioned included those who had been physically emasculated by surgery, a not uncommon practice in the ancient world. In the ancient world eunuchs had charge of the royal harem because of their unquestioned fidelity.

The third group, however, requires particular attention—"eunuchs who made themselves eunuchs for the sake of the kingdom of heaven" (19:12). This concept was tragically misunderstood and interpreted literally in the early Christian centuries. The great theologian Origen (AD 185–254) took the drastic step of self-mutilation in hope of avoiding temptation and sexual sin. However, by the fourth century the church adopted rules permanently barring from the ministry those who had emasculated themselves.

Quite clearly Jesus was speaking here about those who for the sake of furthering the kingdom chose to forgo marriage. God enables certain individuals to remain single, voluntarily choosing a celibate lifestyle in order to devote themselves to God's work.

But others are single because of various circumstances—single again because of divorce, single again because of the death of a spouse. They can make a significant contribution to our churches and the kingdom. Still others, for a variety of reasons, choose to remain single. Since singles are a part of the church family, ministering to the single should be a vital focus for any church.

The Blessing of the Children (19:13–15)

Years ago I heard someone make an incisive statement that has stuck in my mind. He said, "You never know to whom you are speaking when you speak to a child." That hyperactive ten-year-old may be the next generation's Billy

Graham. Or that little boy or girl you saw at the water fountain may become President of the United States. That is why this brief three-verse record of Jesus blessing the children is such a moving event.

Evidently the parents of these children, recognizing the kindness and warmth of Jesus, were bringing them for a blessing. To bring a child to the elders on the evening of the Day of Atonement was a well-known Jewish custom. Perhaps this is the background of this occasion.

Why did the Twelve try to prevent this? Perhaps they felt that Jesus had more important matters at hand, or possibly they saw this as an interruption to his teaching. Whom did the Twelve rebuke, the parents or the children? The phrasing of Matthew is simply, "the disciples rebuked *them*" (19:13, italics for emphasis). If indeed the children were being rebuked, we see quite a clash of attitudes between Jesus and the disciples!

> *The attitude and actions of Jesus toward children should be reflected in our lives and the life of our churches.*

But the Twelve misjudged Jesus. Mark recorded that he was "indignant" (Mark 10:14) at the Twelve. He commanded that they stop hindering the children. So we have the beautiful picture of the Lord placing his hands on these little ones, praying for them and blessing them.

Note the wording of Matthew 19:14: "for the kingdom of heaven belongs to such as these." With this statement Jesus looked beyond the children to others who would come to him with a childlike spirit and attitude. Children recognize their dependence on others. Children are without prejudice, and they are quick to forgive. Children exercise faith so very easily.

Our society often places little value on children. We fail to protect them and to properly evaluate their potential. The attitude and actions of Jesus toward children should be reflected in our lives and the life of our churches. Bringing children to learn of Christ and ultimately place their faith in him should be a priority. We should recognize the value of children to the kingdom as well as to the family.

QUESTIONS

1. What qualities and attitudes give strength and permanence to a marriage? Which of these do you need to address?

2. In the light of Jesus' teachings about divorce, in what ways do we need to reevaluate both marriage and divorce?

3. Does your church need to strengthen its ministry to singles? How can you help?

4. Does your church need to strengthen its ministry to children? How can you help?

5. Does your church affirm the value of children and young people in its allocation of funds and personnel?

6. What does Jesus' attitude toward children say about the priorities of a church regarding children and young people?

NOTES

1. The Barna Research Group conducted the survey in early 2000.

Focal Text
Matthew 25:31–46

Background
Matthew 23—25

Main Focus
Christians must be ready for God to judge the genuineness of their faith by their deeds of mercy and kindness to people in need.

Study Aim
To decide what actions you should take to demonstrate the genuineness of your faith

Question to Explore
What place do actions of mercy and kindness toward people in need have in your life?

Texts Priorities Emphasized

Texas Priorities Emphasized
- Share the gospel of Jesus Christ with the people of Texas, the nation, and the world
- Minister to human needs in the name of Jesus Christ
- Equip people for ministry in the church and in the world

LESSON ELEVEN

Are You Ready?

Quick Read
With the return of Christ, he will judge all people, dividing them into two groups. The basis of judgment and the proof that the righteous loved Christ will be their ministry to others.

Does the gospel have social consequences? Ask Tillie Burgin that question and you will get a resounding, "Yes!" Texas Baptists can be justly proud of her leadership of "Mission Arlington" and its remarkable outreach to Christians and non-Christians alike. Mrs. Burgin, the minister of missions at First Baptist Church, Arlington, and the director of Mission Arlington, is the founder and prime mover of that ministry. Operating with church benevolence funds, the original plan was to establish Bible studies to draw people to the church and do benevolence and apartment ministry. But a telephone call rewrote the plan and was the beginning of Mission Arlington. The call was from a woman in an Arlington apartment complex who needed help in paying her electric bill. Mrs. Burgin visited her, offered the help the woman needed, and asked whether she could have a Bible study in the apartment. The woman agreed, but she noted that she had no furniture for people to use during the study. Mrs. Burgin secured the furniture, found a teacher for the study, and the ministry began with seventeen people.

Word began to spread of the positive impact the Bible study had on behavior in the apartment complex. Soon six Bible studies were going as apartment complex managers began to open their doors—and, as the saying goes, the rest is history.

The statistics reflecting the outreach of Mission Arlington are phenomenal. Now 215 weekly Bible studies attended by 3,700 people are held in apartment complexes, mobile home parks, retirement centers, nursing homes, office buildings, and private residences. In addition:

- 42,000 families and 189,000 individuals are helped each year.
- 2,500 patients are seen annually in a state-of-the-art free dental clinic.
- 2,200 patients are treated annually in a free medical clinic.
- 50 children of homeless and at-risk families are cared for daily.
- 650 children each week participate in after-school programs at 26 sites.
- 2,000 volunteers work at Mission Arlington, not including more than 100 out-of-town mission groups numbering 2,000 people from more than 18 states and more than 1,000 assigned by legal entities to do community service.

This is but a sample of the ministry being done in the name of Christ. Yet a sign in the reception area of the headquarters building focuses all the efforts. It reads, "The only help you will receive here that lasts forever is Jesus."

Matthew 25:31–46

[31]"But when the Son of Man comes in His glory, and all the angels with Him, then He will sit on His glorious throne. [32]"All the nations will be gathered before Him; and He will separate them from one another, as the shepherd separates the sheep from the goats; [33]and He will put the sheep on His right, and the goats on the left.

[34]"Then the King will say to those on His right, 'Come, you who are blessed of My Father, inherit the kingdom prepared for you from the foundation of the world. [35]'For I was hungry, and you gave Me something to eat; I was thirsty, and you gave Me something to drink; I was a stranger, and you invited Me in; [36]naked, and you clothed Me; I was sick, and you visited Me; I was in prison, and you came to Me.' [37]"Then the righteous will answer Him, 'Lord, when did we see You hungry, and feed You, or thirsty, and give You something to drink? [38]'And when did we see You a stranger, and invite You in, or naked, and clothe You? [39]'When did we see You sick, or in prison, and come to You?' [40]"The King will answer and say to them, 'Truly I say to you, to the extent that you did it to one of these brothers of Mine, even the least of them, you did it to Me.'

[41]"Then He will also say to those on His left, 'Depart from Me, accursed ones, into the eternal fire which has been prepared for the devil and his angels; [42]for I was hungry, and you gave Me nothing to eat; I was thirsty, and you gave Me nothing to drink; [43]I was a stranger, and you did not invite Me in; naked, and you did not clothe Me; sick, and in prison, and you did not visit Me.' [44]"Then they themselves also will answer, 'Lord, when did we see You hungry, or thirsty, or a stranger, or naked, or sick, or in prison, and did not take care of You?' [45]"Then He will answer them, 'Truly I say to you, to the extent that you did not do it to one of the least of these, you did not do it to Me.' [46]"These will go away into eternal punishment, but the righteous into eternal life."

The Setting

Matthew 25:31–46 comprises the last section of the fifth major discourse recorded in Matthew's Gospel. In chapter 23, Matthew recorded Jesus' scathing rebuke of the scribes and Pharisees, religious leaders who had opposed his ministry from its beginning. Describing their hypocrisy, Jesus had condemned their petty legalism and self-serving false piety. Judgment was coming, he declared, telling them "Behold, your house is being left to you desolate"—that is, deserted, devoid of aid (23:38).

Chapters 24—25 form what is known as the Olivet Discourse. In response to the comments of the Twelve about the magnificence of Herod's Temple, Jesus used apocalyptic terminology to speak of coming judgment. The overwhelming majority of Bible students recognize that he was speaking prophetically of two events—the destruction of the temple by the Romans in AD 70 and his own second coming. The focal text for the lesson today pictures Christ's return and his judging all people.

> *This passage by no means suggests that salvation is the result of the good works we might do.*

Is this a parable? In the first part of chapter 25, Jesus had told two parables, the parable of the ten virgins (25:1–13) and the parable of the talents (25:14–30). However, this narrative in 25:31–46 is not based on a fictitious story but on the description of a very real future event. Although some elements used in parables are included, the future tense forms employed lead us to characterize this as apocalyptic revelation discourse. The most striking feature of these verses is the four-fold repetition of six needs. In each repeating of the needs the terms are the same and the order of the terms does not change.

The Coming of the Son of Man (25:31)

Jesus spoke of himself as the Son of Man. This is the title that Jesus used most often when speaking of himself. Because the terms used for the Messiah by the Jewish people in the first century had unfortunate political connotations, Jesus chose a different term. Found in Psalms, Ezekiel, and Daniel, the title "Son of Man" was chosen by Jesus so that he could be free to fill it with his own meaning about himself as the Messiah. He thus avoided the political baggage of the more commonly used messianic designations.

Jesus spoke of this coming "in His glory" (25:31). He would be accompanied by the angels, and he would sit on "His glorious throne" (25:31). Jesus' first coming was by worldly standards quite inglorious. This second coming, however, would in contrast be majestic and powerful. At Jesus' first coming, people could easily reject him, but kingly authority would mark his second coming. All would be required to stand before him. In his first coming, he was associated with a manger and a cross. In his second coming, he would be associated with a throne and a crown.

The Great Separation (25:32–33)

The identity of "all the nations" (25:32) has been a matter of differing opinions. Some suggest that this is one of a series of judgments, that it is a judgment of nations not individuals, and that the basis of judgment will be how these nations have treated the Jewish people. Others point out that "all the nations" is the same all-inclusive phrase used in Matthew 28:19, the Great Commission. Too, the judgment shifts quickly from the neuter "nations" to the masculine "them" (25:32b), suggesting that individuals rather than nations or people groups are intended.

Redemption was in the heart of God long before sin was in the heart of humankind.

Those standing before the One on the throne will be separated as a shepherd separates sheep from goats. Quite normally sheep and goats mingled during the day, but at night they were often separated. The simile of "sheep" is often used in the Old Testament for God's people, and indeed Matthew reflected this in 10:16; 26:31. The *right* and *left* in Jewish thought and in that of other cultures designated favor and disfavor, good and bad fortune. For those on the right there will be reward; for those on the left, judgment.

The Reward of the Righteous (25:34–40)

The Son of Man is now the *King*, the one sitting on the throne and proceeding to pronounce judgment. His invitation is, "Come, you who are blessed of My Father" (25:34). The specific word translated "blessed" described the righteous now taking their inheritance. The inheritance becomes theirs because they have a relationship with the Father.

Does the gospel have social consequences?

They are to inherit "the kingdom" (25:34). If he is the *king*, though, what sort of *kingdom* do they inherit? Jesus had previously indicated (19:28) that his followers would share his kingly authority. So it is possible that the language here means they now share his kingly authority. This kingdom is one "prepared" for them, that is, secured for them through the redemptive work of God in Christ (25:34). While chronologically the cross was yet in the future and not yet an historical fact, Jesus was always "the Lamb slain from the foundation of the world"

125

(Revelation 13:8, KJV). The event that was in the heart of God in eternity would with certainty become an actual historical fact. Redemption was in the heart of God long before sin was in the heart of humankind. God's eternal purpose was now to be accomplished.

Jesus now cited the reason for their admission to the kingdom, and it is more evidential than causative. This passage by no means suggests that salvation is the result of the good works we might do. Six acts of mercy are named by the King. "I was hungry" is the first (Matt. 25:35). This is the word used by Jesus in the Beatitudes (5:6). It reflects an avid desire for food. "I was thirsty" is mentioned next (25:35). According to the common oriental view, to give a drink to the thirsty was a work of practical assistance that was especially pleasing to God. Figuratively the term was used to describe a passionate desire for that which sustains life.

"I was a stranger" calls for special attention (25:35). Foreigners were often treated poorly in the first century. The papyri, which contain writings from everyday life in the ancient world, record the account of a man who wrote home saying that he was despised by everyone "because I am a stranger." To treat a stranger with kindness was a sign of a godly character.

To be "naked" is the fourth need noted (25:36). The word often means a person who has only an undergarment rather than one who is completely unclothed.

Being "sick" (25:36) in the first century when medical knowledge was primitive and laced with superstition might speak of a desperate condition.

Texas Baptist Human Welfare Ministries

In 1877 Dr. R.C. Buckner began the first child care institution for Texas Baptists, and a ministry to the aged followed shortly thereafter.[2] The first Texas Baptist hospital was founded by Dr. Buckner, Dr. George W. Truett, Colonel C.C. Slaughter, and others in Dallas in 1903.[3] Other similar institutions soon began to spring up over Texas until today there is a network of Baptist hospitals, childcare institutions, and homes for the aged across the state.

In a recent year these Texas Baptist institutions provided care to more than 2.6 million people. Hospitals provide treatment in an atmosphere of Christian compassion. Retirement centers continue to grow as the population of our state ages. Further, in a recent year, children's homes provided care for more than 37,000 children and members of their families. Much of this care was focused on prevention ministry to families and children.

The word "visited" in relation to illness means more than a mere visit. It included as well looking after the sick (25:36).

The last of the six needs was being "in prison." In both the Old and New Testaments, imprisonment was a common fate of the righteous. Remember that the prisons of that day had very little in common with prisons of our day.

Jesus now cited the reason for their admission to the kingdom, and it is more evidential than causative.

Verses 37–39 reflect the surprise of the righteous. They were astonished at the statement of Jesus, having taken quite literally that they had ministered to his needs. Their three-fold question revealed that they could not remember a circumstance when they had ministered to him. Their confusion gave rise to the articulation of an astounding principle, that in ministering to "one of these brothers of mine, even the least of them, you did it to Me" (25:40).

Who are these "brothers of mine"? Bible students differ in their identification of this group. Consider several possible approaches:

- Most commentators understand them to be all who are hungry, needy, and in distress. Kingdom citizens, it is suggested, are those who openly manifest deeds of mercy and compassion. Many authors cite the Jewish parallels relating to compassion and almsgiving.
- A second approach holds that three mutually exclusive groups are involved: those outside the Christian community who think they are part of it; those inside the community but not the "little ones"; and the rest of the Christian community. The attitude of believers toward the "little ones" becomes the basis for judgement.

To treat a stranger with kindness was a sign of a godly character.

- Another approach sees this as a reference to the Lord's return following the removal of the church by the rapture. Jesus' "brothers" are Jews converted during the tribulation, and the "nations" consist of converted Gentiles. The judgment is for the purpose of deciding which nations will become a part of the millennial kingdom. This view is held primarily by those of a dispensational persuasion.
- A fourth suggestion holds that Jesus' "brothers" are his disciples, including Christian missionaries and Christian leaders. Because of their determination to follow Christ at any cost, they have been

and will be subjected to hunger, thirst, imprisonment, and the other needs mentioned. Good deeds done to the Lord's followers as they spread the gospel are seen as works of compassion for the Lord himself.[1]

The Judgment of the Wicked (25:41–45)

The condemnation of the wicked, those on the king's left hand, is now addressed. The wicked were to "depart" from him (25:41). This sentence reminds us of the judgment pictured in Matthew 7:23, and both pictures reflect Psalm 6:8. Jesus addressed the wicked as "accursed ones." They are consigned to "eternal fire" (25:41). Jesus often used the word *gehenna*, the garbage dump of Jerusalem, as a figure of hell. Although the specific word *gehenna* is not used here, that seems to be the intent. A valley southeast of the city of Jerusalem, *gehenna* was known as a place where fire was always burning.

We noted that the kingdom had been prepared for the righteous. Observe that eternal fire had *not* been prepared for the unrighteous. Rather, eternal fire "has been prepared for the devil and his angels" (25:41). Tragically, the word "eternal" modifies this punishment reserved for the unrighteous.

Notice in 25:42–43 that the King consigned the wicked to their punishment because they had *not* done the very things that the righteous had done. Nothing is said here about vicious or angry activity, just what they had failed to do. Have you heard your grandparents pray about sins of "omission and commission"? Well, here are the sins of omission, good things that should have been done but that were left undone. What an arresting declaration from the heart of James, "Therefore to one who knows the right thing to do, and does not do it, to him it is sin" (James 4:17). The same six needs are cited in 25:42–43 as in 25:35–36, but this time they were unmet.

Acts of service to the needy, and especially to the household of faith, must demonstrate our allegiance to the Lord Jesus.

As the righteous were surprised at the judgment of the King, so also were the wicked. To their questioning Jesus responded with a parallel reply. The fact that "brothers" is omitted from verse 45 is merely an abridgment and should not be considered a change of emphasis from the phrase in verse 40.

The Final Division (25:46)

The last sentence of the passage underscores the final separation of the two groups. The destiny of the one group is "eternal punishment," and the destiny of the other is "eternal life." The adjective "eternal" is used to modify both conditions. Some interpreters see annihilationism in these verses. Annihilationism is the notion that people are simply annihilated into unconscious nothingness in the punishment, with the punishment thus being limited. To see any notion of annihilationism in "eternal punishment" is quite difficult, however. To place a limit on the "eternal punishment" is to place a limit on the "eternal life."

Our Lord's mandate is quite clear. Since there are only two kinds of people in the world and only two places of eternal destiny, we must respond properly to needs we observe. Acts of service to the needy, and especially to the household of faith, must demonstrate our allegiance to the Lord Jesus.

QUESTIONS

1. Are we saved by grace or by works? What is the relationship of the two? What does Scripture teach?

2. What do Jesus' statements about meeting the needs of others say to you?

3. Is there a situation of need in your church family that you personally should address?

NOTES

1. D.A. Carson, "Matthew," *The Expositor's Bible Commentary* (Grand Rapids: Zondervan, 1984), VIII: 519–520.
2. Harry Leon McBeth, *Texas Baptists: A Sesquicentennial History* (Dallas: BAPTISTWAY PRESS®, 1998), 108–110.
3. McBeth, *Texas Baptists*, 138.

Jesus' Destiny and Ours

Each gospel devotes from one-fourth to one-third of its material to the events of the last week of Jesus' earthly ministry. Indeed, the climax of each gospel is the crucifixion and resurrection of Jesus, and this is true of Matthew's Gospel as of the other three. The heart of the gospel message is found in these two truths: Christ died for our sins as our substitute on the cross, and he arose on the third day as the victor over death and the grave. The crucifixion and the resurrection are like two sides of a coin; one is not complete without the other. The crucifixion without the resurrection is only half of the story.

Two most significant lessons comprise this unit, covering Matthew 26—28. The first lesson, from Matthew 26—27, examines the crucifixion experience and the death of Jesus on our behalf. Two events that preceded the crucifixion—the establishment of the Lord's Supper and the agony in the Garden of Gethsemane—will be considered. But the central focus of this lesson is on the six hours Jesus spent on the cross, dying in our place. The second lesson, from Matthew 28, recounts the resurrection of Jesus, along with the amazement and joy of the followers of Jesus. Matthew 28:19–20, the Great Commission, will require our special attention.[1]

The lessons will permit us to relive with Jesus several of the most important events in human history, including these:

- Jesus' last meal with the Twelve and why we celebrate the Lord's Supper
- The battle that was settled in Gethsemane and its implications for us
- The cruel price that was paid for our salvation
- The victory and promise of the resurrection
- The foremost command that Jesus gave us

Lesson 12   The Gift We Can't Live Without   Matthew 26:26–29,
                                                   36–45; 27:33–55

Lesson 13   The Command We Dare Not Ignore   Matthew 28:1–10,
                                                   16–20

NOTES

1. Unless otherwise indicated, all Scripture quotes in Unit 6, Lessons 12–13, are from the New American Standard Bible®.

Focal Text

Matthew
26:26–29,36–45;
27:33–55

Background

Matthew 26—27

Main Focus

Jesus gave his life for
the forgiveness of our
sins.

Study Aim

To summarize the
meaning for my life of
Jesus' giving his life on
the cross

Question to Explore

What does Jesus' giving his life mean to you?

Texas Priorities Emphasized

- Share the gospel of Jesus Christ with the people of Texas, the nation, and the world

LESSON TWELVE

The Gift We Can't Live Without

Quick Read

In the crucifixion of Jesus, God came to grips with our greatest problem: the problem of sin. Through his crucifixion, Jesus gave his life for the forgiveness of our sins. Two significant events leading up to the crucifixion are the institution of the Lord's Supper and the Gethsemane experience.

"Who Killed Jesus?" That question served as the title for one of the most gripping sermons I have ever heard.[1]

In the message the preacher detailed the individuals and groups who contributed to the crucifixion of Jesus. He first mentioned Judas, who with a kiss betrayed Jesus into the hands of his enemies. Then he named Caiaphas the high priest, who hatched the plot to do away with Jesus. Third, he noted the crowd who blindly followed the urging of the religious leaders. The preacher made a striking observation in a statement that God himself somehow caused the death of Jesus, for the Father's purpose from eternity was that the Son should pay the penalty for the sins of humankind. Then the preacher commented that in answering the question, we should remember that Jesus said, "No one has taken it [my life] away from Me, but I lay it down on My own initiative" (John 10:18). The sermon's most moving point was the final and climactic one. The preacher said, "But if you will examine the mallet that drove the spikes into his hands and feet, you will find your fingerprints on it, for it was your sins that placed him on the cross!"

That is more than sermonic imagery, for it is true that your sins—and mine—put Jesus on the cross of Calvary. Not one of us can plead innocent; we were all involved.

With the events of chapter 26, Matthew began to describe the plot being developed to do away with Jesus. The high priest Caiaphas, whom the Jewish historian Josephus called a "sly and rude manipulator," led the Jewish religious leaders in their diabolical planning (Matt. 26:3–4). After mentioning the plotting that was occurring, Matthew then related the beautiful story of the devotion of Mary of Bethany and her anointing Jesus at the supper in the home of Simon the leper (26:6–13). The plot against Jesus thickened as Judas went to the chief priests, precipitating the bargain to betray the Lord (26:14–16). The gospels give us no record of the happenings on Wednesday, often called "The Day of Silence." The gospels next describe the preparation for the Feast of Passover that would be celebrated on Thursday evening (see 26:17–19). Our focal text begins with what happened as Jesus and the disciples celebrated the feast, an event that has become known to us as the Last Supper.

In the Upper Room (26:26–30)

During the Passover Feast, Jesus instituted the Lord's Supper. What shall we call this meal celebrated by all Christians? Shall we call it communion?

Matthew 26:26–29,36–45

26While they were eating, Jesus took some bread, and after a blessing, He broke it and gave it to the disciples, and said, "Take, eat; this is My body." 27And when He had taken a cup and given thanks, He gave it to them, saying, "Drink from it, all of you; 28for this is My blood of the covenant, which is poured out for many for forgiveness of sins. 29"But I say to you, I will not drink of this fruit of the vine from now on until that day when I drink it new with you in My Father's kingdom."

•••

36Then Jesus came with them to a place called Gethsemane, and said to His disciples, "Sit here while I go over there and pray." 37And He took with Him Peter and the two sons of Zebedee, and began to be grieved and distressed. 38Then He said to them, "My soul is deeply grieved, to the point of death; remain here and keep watch with Me."

39And He went a little beyond them, and fell on His face and prayed, saying, "My Father, if it is possible, let this cup pass from Me; yet not as I will, but as You will." 40And He came to the disciples and found them sleeping, and said to Peter, "So, you men could not keep watch with Me for one hour? 41"Keep watching and praying that you may not enter into temptation; the spirit is willing, but the flesh is weak."

42He went away again a second time and prayed, saying, "My Father, if this cannot pass away unless I drink it, Your will be done." 43Again He came and found them sleeping, for their eyes were heavy. 44And He left them again, and went away and prayed a third time, saying the same thing once more. 45Then He came to the disciples and said to them, "Are you still sleeping and resting? Behold, the hour is at hand and the Son of Man is being betrayed into the hands of sinners.

Matthew 27:33–55

33And when they came to a place called Golgotha, which means Place of a Skull, 34they gave Him wine to drink mixed with gall; and after tasting it, He was unwilling to drink.

35And when they had crucified Him, they divided up His garments among themselves by casting lots. 36And sitting down, they began to keep watch over Him there. 37And above His head they put up the charge against Him which read, "THIS IS JESUS THE KING OF THE JEWS."

38At that time two robbers were crucified with Him, one on the right and one on the left. 39And those passing by were hurling abuse at Him, wagging their heads ⁴⁰and saying, "You who are going to destroy the temple and rebuild it in three days, save Yourself! If You are the Son of God, come down from the cross." ⁴¹In the same way the chief priests also, along with the scribes and elders, were mocking Him and saying, ⁴²"He saved others; He cannot save Himself. He is the King of Israel; let Him now come down from the cross, and we will believe in Him. ⁴³"HE TRUSTS IN GOD; LET GOD RESCUE Him now, IF HE DELIGHTS IN HIM; for He said, 'I am the Son of God.'" ⁴⁴The robbers who had been crucified with Him were also insulting Him with the same words.

⁴⁵Now from the sixth hour darkness fell upon all the land until the ninth hour. ⁴⁶About the ninth hour Jesus cried out with a loud voice, saying, "ELI, ELI, LAMA SABACHTHANI?" that is, "MY GOD, MY GOD, WHY HAVE YOU FORSAKEN ME?" ⁴⁷And some of those who were standing there, when they heard it, began saying, "This man is calling for Elijah." ⁴⁸Immediately one of them ran, and taking a sponge, he filled it with sour wine and put it on a reed, and gave Him a drink. ⁴⁹But the rest of them said, "Let us see whether Elijah will come to save Him." ⁵⁰And Jesus cried out again with a loud voice, and yielded up His spirit. ⁵¹And behold, the veil of the temple was torn in two from top to bottom; and the earth shook and the rocks were split. ⁵²The tombs were opened, and many bodies of the saints who had fallen asleep were raised; ⁵³and coming out of the tombs after His resurrection they entered the holy city and appeared to many. ⁵⁴Now the centurion, and those who were with him keeping guard over Jesus, when they saw the earthquake and the things that were happening, became very frightened and said, "Truly this was the Son of God!"

⁵⁵Many women were there looking on from a distance, who had followed Jesus from Galilee while ministering to Him.

This is a perfectly good term so long as we remember that the communion is vertical not horizontal: it is for communion with the Lord Himself, not merely with fellow believers. Shall we call it the Lord's Supper? This is the term preferred and used by most Baptists, underscoring the fact that Jesus established it as a memorial meal to remind us of his death and his return.

Both Mark and Luke tell us that the Passover Feast was held in an "upper room" (Mark 14:15; Luke 22:11). The Passover Feast was celebrated in order to remind the Jewish people of God's delivering their ancestors from Egyptian slavery and from the visit of the death angel. However, Jesus chose to use this occasion to initiate a new meal that would speak of an even greater deliverance. During the meal he took the

Passover bread, broke it, blessed it, and gave the pieces to the disciples. Then he took a cup, gave thanks, and shared it also (26:27). Of the "fruit of the vine" (26:29) he said, "This is my blood of the covenant" (26:28). He thus echoed the prophecy of Jeremiah 31:31–34 that a new covenant would be established.

> *. . . Your sins—and mine— put Jesus on the cross of Calvary.*

It is unfortunate that this simple act and the symbolism of the meal have been so tragically misinterpreted. The meal is not a means of grace; it is a memorial. It is not some mystical happening that causes the bread and wine to become Jesus' body and blood; it is symbolic. So Baptists celebrate the Lord's Supper as a memorial meal, with the bread and the cup serving as symbols of our Lord's death on our behalf, reminding us as well of his return.

In the Garden of Gethsemane (26:36–45)

After finishing the Passover meal, Jesus and the eleven disciples walked to the Mount of Olives. Judas had left earlier (John 13:30). The Mount of Olives was located just east of the city of Jerusalem and the temple area. Probably during their walk toward the Mount of Olives, Jesus quoted Zechariah 14:7, predicting that the disciples would desert him in his hour of greatest crisis (see Matt. 26:31). When Peter declared that he would be faithful whatever happened, Jesus predicted his threefold denial (26:33–34).

> *Baptists celebrate the Lord's Supper as a memorial meal, with the bread and the cup serving as symbols of our Lord's death on our behalf, reminding us as well of his return.*

Located on the Mount of Olives was an olive grove, the Garden of Gethsemane. *Gethsemane* is an Aramaic word meaning *olive press*. Evidently Gethsemane was a quiet and secluded place. Jesus likely had gone there often with the Twelve.

Leaving eight of the disciples at one place, Jesus took Peter, James, and John with him a bit farther. Significantly, these three had all declared their determination to be faithful to Jesus whatever the cost (20:22; 26:35). Matthew records that Jesus "began to be grieved and distressed" (26:37). The Phillips translation of the New Testament catches the force of these words, translating them, "began to be in terrible distress and misery."[2]

Crucifixion

Crucifixion is the most cruel, painful, and shameful manner of execution that people have ever developed to kill their fellow human beings. The Persians evidently originated crucifixion. The Greeks under Alexander the Great adopted this method of execution, especially after his conquest of Tyre. When the Romans adopted crucifixion, they considered it so violent that only slaves, never citizens or freeborn, were subject to it.

This penalty was considered by Roman governors to be an effective deterrent for crime, especially sedition. The condemned person was usually flogged first and then forced to carry the crossbeam to the place of execution. He was fastened to the beam, sometimes with ropes, sometimes with spikes. Then the body and the beam were lifted into place and attached to the upright. With one spike the feet were attached to the upright. Usually death was caused by suffocation brought about by fatigue, but a person often survived for thirty-six to forty-eight hours.

Jesus said to the three disciples, "My soul is deeply grieved, to the point of death" (26:38). These words indicate clearly Jesus' awareness of the approaching experience of death. Going farther into the garden, he prostrated himself and began to pray to the Father. Mark's Gospel reveals the depth of the agony involved, using the words "Abba! Father!" (Mark 14:36). *Abba* is the Aramaic term that a child would use in addressing his father.

Jesus' prayer concerned "this cup," and the essence of the prayer was that he be delivered from drinking it (Matt. 26:39). What was "this cup"? Some suggest that Jesus was asking that innocent individuals not be held responsible for the awful crime of his crucifixion—like the soldiers, for instance. A better possibility is that "this cup" represented his death on the cross and everything that would be involved in it. He did not cringe from just physical death, although death by crucifixion was indeed horrible. He shrank from the spiritual implications of his crucifixion in which he would become sin for humankind and would experience separation from the Father.

Returning to the three disciples and finding them asleep, Jesus went away a second time and then a third time to pray a similar prayer. Jesus' prayer, "yet not as I will, but as You will," must be underscored (26:39). Throughout the entire agonizing ordeal, Jesus voiced his willingness to see the Father's will carried out.

On the Cross (27:33–55)

The four gospels tell us that Jesus was arrested in the garden following Judas' kiss of betrayal. Peter attempted to defend Jesus with a sword, cutting off the ear of a servant of the high priest (27:51; see John 18:10). Although misguided, Peter's courage was evident in the face of the considerable number of soldiers, perhaps 200 or more. Three Jewish trials, or hearings, followed, first before Annas, then before Caiaphas, and finally before the entire Sanhedrin. Since an execution required the approval of the Roman governor, Jesus was taken to Pontius Pilate, appeared briefly before Herod Antipas, and then was officially condemned to death by Pilate. After being scourged and ridiculed by the Roman soldiers, Jesus was led away to be crucified.

Throughout the entire agonizing ordeal, Jesus voiced his willingness to see the Father's will carried out.

The crucifixion of Jesus took place at a location called Golgotha, a name that comes from an Aramaic word meaning "skull." The name probably came from a pre-Christian tradition that the skull of Adam was found here. Origen, an early Christian leader and scholar (AD 185–254), first mentioned this concept. As far-fetched as the tradition is, this is the most ancient explanation.

Just prior to the crucifixion, Jesus was offered "wine to drink, mingled with gall" (Matt. 27:34). Gall was a narcotic given to dull the excruciating pain of crucifixion. But Jesus refused it, choosing rather to face the experience with his mind entirely clear. When Jesus had been placed on the cross, the soldiers divided his garments among themselves, casting lots for his seamless robe (27:35). Little did they realize that in that act they were fulfilling Old Testament prophecy (Psalm 22:18).

It was precisely because he was not willing to save himself that he was able to bring about the salvation of others.

Matthew tells us that a sign was placed above Jesus' head, "This is Jesus the King of the Jews" (27:37). John's Gospel tells us that Pilate was the author of the wording (John 19:19–20). Pilate stipulated that the sign be written in three languages—Hebrew, Latin, and Greek. It is significant that Hebrew was the language of religion, Latin the language of government, and Greek the language of culture. All three entities had a part in placing Jesus there. John also tells us that the Jewish religious leaders appealed to Pilate and asked that it read, "He said, 'I am King of the Jews'" (19:21). But Pilate stubbornly responded, "What I have written I have written" (19:22).

Matthew recorded also that the religious leaders taunted Jesus (Matt. 27:41). It seems unthinkable that mature, religious people would do such a shameful thing, but such is the extreme to which evil will go! What they said in mocking Jesus is most ironic, "He saved others; He cannot save Himself" (27:42). Their statement was hauntingly true. It was precisely because he was not willing to save himself that he was able to bring about the salvation of others.

Two robbers were crucified along with Jesus, one on either side. They joined in the jeers from Jesus' enemies, according to Matthew, "insulting Him with the same words" (27:44). Luke recorded, however, that one of the robbers began to realize that there was something strikingly different about Jesus (Luke 23:40–41).

Jesus was on the cross for six hours, from 9:00 a.m. to 3:00 p.m. (See Matt. 27:45; Mark 15:25.) At noon there came an eerie darkness over the land. It is indeed fitting that the Father shielded the Son from the curious eyes of the crowd as Jesus paid the penalty for the sins of humankind. About 3:00 p.m., Jesus cried out in Hebrew/Aramaic (Matt. 27:46), "'My God, My God, why have You forsaken Me?'" His words reflected the question found in Psalm 22:1.

Jesus was forsaken that we might not be forsaken.

How shall we understand this cry spoken in agony? To say that Jesus was experiencing an awful loneliness is to touch only the hem of the garment. Realize that sin begins when one forsakes God, and sin ends in "God-forsakenness." Jesus at this mysterious moment was experiencing the end result of sin: being forsaken by God. He was at this point bearing the penalty of

Application Actions

- Some churches ask various families in the church to prepare the unleavened bread for the Lord's Supper observance. Would the event be more significant if you were involved in the preparation?
- Consider doing additional research into the history and details of crucifixion to help you to be more aware of the agony experienced by our Lord in his crucifixion.

humankind's sins for each one of us. As Paul phrased it, "He made Him who knew no sin to be sin on our behalf, so that we might become the righteousness of God in Him" (2 Corinthians 5:21). Jesus was forsaken that we might not be forsaken. He experienced the agony of hell so that we might not experience it.

We must realize that God the Father was never so much at work in the world as he was in that moment when God the Son was paying the penalty for our sins.

A story told of Martin Luther, the great Protestant reformer, is that on one occasion he determined to attempt to grasp the full meaning of Jesus' question about being forsaken by the Father. He went into his study and dimmed the lights a bit. For three hours he read, prayed, and thought, trying to determine what all was involved in Jesus' question. At the end of those three hours, in exasperation he leaped to his feet, flung his arms in the air, and cried out, "God forsaken of God! Who can understand that?" And perhaps we must reach the same conclusion. We must realize that God the Father was never so much at work in the world as he was in that moment when God the Son was paying the penalty for our sins.

With the struggle finished, Jesus said, "'I am thirsty'" (John 19:28). Someone soaked a sponge in the cheap wine the soldiers bought and lifted it up to Jesus' mouth. Having drunk the wine, Jesus cried out in victory, "It is finished!" (19:30). The word in the Greek text is a perfect tense verb, a tense that conveys the idea of completed action with continuing results. So the word could be translated, *It stands done!* Jesus did not say *I am finished*, but rather he said, "It is finished." He was declaring that the redemptive work designed by the Father in eternity past had been completed.

How have you responded to Jesus' giving his life on the cross for you?

Matthew records that "Jesus cried out again with a loud voice, and yielded up His spirit" (Matt. 27:50). Luke provides additional details, recording that Jesus said, "'Father, into Your hands I commit my spirit'" (Luke 23:46). Two elements about this statement are important. First, it was a voluntary act; Jesus at this moment dismissed his spirit, permitting it to return to the Father. Indeed no one had taken Jesus' life from him; he dismissed it. Second, this was a conscious act. In full control of the situation, Jesus said essentially, *The work is done; now take me home!* What a splendid light this throws on the death of any Christian! For us, too, death is not our master to be feared, but rather it is our servant to transport us to the Father's house.

Three strange events took place when Jesus died. Note first that the veil in the temple was split "from top to bottom" (Matt. 27:51). This huge thick veil separated the Holy Place from the Holy of Holies. The author of Hebrews would later interpret this as indicating that the way into the presence of God was now open, "by a new and living way which He inaugurated for us through the veil, that is, His flesh" (Hebrews 10:20). Note second that "the earth shook, and the rocks were split" (Matt. 27:51). Note third that graves were opened, and after the resurrection of Jesus raised saints appeared in Jerusalem (27:52–53). This account appears only in Matthew, and many unanswered questions remain. Matthew recorded the phenomenon probably to demonstrate the far-reaching power of Jesus' resurrection. And that is next week's study—the resurrection of Jesus.

For You

As you consider this portion of Scripture, remember that what happened was for you. How have you responded to Jesus' giving his life on the cross for you?

QUESTIONS

1. Since partaking of the Lord's Supper is such a serious and symbolic occasion, what should be the attitude of a Christian as he or she approaches the observance?

2. What does the prayer of Jesus in the Garden of Gethsemane say to you about how you as a Christian should pray?

3. What attitudes of the Jewish religious leaders led them to seek the execution of Jesus? Do you find any of these in your life?

4. What are the implications for your life of the torn veil in the temple?

NOTES

1. The preacher was Dr. G. Earl Guinn.
2. The New Testament in Modern English, trans. J.B. Phillips (New York: The Macmillan Company, 1964).

Question to Explore
How well are we demonstrating belief in Jesus' resurrection?

Texas Priorities Emphasized
- Share the gospel of Jesus Christ with the people of Texas, the nation, and the world

LESSON THIRTEEN

The Command We Dare Not Ignore

Quick Read
At first startled and amazed when they realized the reality of the resurrection, the disciples of Jesus soon reacted with joy and gratitude. Jesus gave them a world-encompassing task in his final command to them.

Two men had the sorrow-filled task of preparing the body of Jesus for burial on that tragic Friday afternoon of the crucifixion. One was Joseph of Arimathea, a man of wealth. A member of the Sanhedrin, he had not agreed with the Sanhedrin's treatment of Jesus. In fact, he had "become a disciple of Jesus" (Matthew 27:57; see John 19:38). Boldly he went to Pilate and requested Jesus' body (Matt. 27:58).

The other man involved in the burial of Jesus was Nicodemus (John 19:39). Also a member of the Sanhedrin, he is best remembered as the man who came to Jesus at night for an opportunity to investigate serious theological questions (3:1). Joining Joseph of Arimathea in preparing Jesus' body, he brought large quantities of expensive spices for the process.

Can you image their conversation as they finished their task, placed Jesus' body in Joseph's tomb, and sealed the tomb with the stone? Joseph may have mused, *I thought he was the Promised One. His miracles astonished me. His words were so fresh and authoritative.* And Nicodemus may have responded, *Yes, I was sure he was God's Messiah. But it's over, he's dead, and that's that.*

But it was not over! Then came Sunday morning!

The truth of the resurrection of Jesus is the cornerstone of the Christian faith. Examine the sermons of the first preachers, and you will hear Peter and Stephen and Paul climaxing their messages with a declaration of the resurrection of Jesus. Examine the lives of the first disciples, and you will find that the resurrection had transformed them from cowards into people of courage.

The climax of each of our four canonical gospels is the account of the resurrection of Jesus. Beginning with our Lord's ancestry and birth and continuing with a summary of the contact with John the Baptist, Matthew had proceeded to give the most complete and extensive account of the teachings of Jesus and to connect Jesus' actions with those teachings. Matthew's Gospel often pictured Jesus with his face toward Jerusalem and the cross. The climactic event of it all is the victory of the resurrection.

The Visit of the Women (28:1–4)

All four gospels indicate that quite early on Sunday morning several women set out to visit the tomb in which the body of Jesus had been placed (28:1; Mark 16:1; Luke 24:1; John 20:1). Their purpose was to

Matthew 28:1–10,16–20

¹Now after the Sabbath, as it began to dawn toward the first day of the week, Mary Magdalene and the other Mary came to look at the grave. ²And behold, a severe earthquake had occurred, for an angel of the Lord descended from heaven and came and rolled away the stone and sat upon it. ³And his appearance was like lightning, and his clothing as white as snow. ⁴The guards shook for fear of him and became like dead men. ⁵The angel said to the women, "Do not be afraid; for I know that you are looking for Jesus who has been crucified. ⁶"He is not here, for He has risen, just as He said. Come, see the place where He was lying. ⁷"Go quickly and tell His disciples that He has risen from the dead; and behold, He is going ahead of you into Galilee, there you will see Him; behold, I have told you."

⁸And they left the tomb quickly with fear and great joy and ran to report it to His disciples. ⁹And behold, Jesus met them and greeted them. And they came up and took hold of His feet and worshiped Him. ¹⁰Then Jesus said to them, "Do not be afraid; go and take word to My brethren to leave for Galilee, and there they will see Me."

• •

¹⁶But the eleven disciples proceeded to Galilee, to the mountain which Jesus had designated. ¹⁷When they saw Him, they worshiped Him; but some were doubtful. ¹⁸And Jesus came up and spoke to them, saying, "All authority has been given to Me in heaven and on earth. ¹⁹"Go therefore and make disciples of all the nations, baptizing them in the name of the Father and the Son and the Holy Spirit, ²⁰teaching them to observe all that I commanded you; and lo, I am with you always, even to the end of the age."

anoint the body of Jesus with spices (Mark 16:1). Quite probably they had purchased these after Sabbath had concluded, that is, late Saturday afternoon. Their early morning journey was not one marked by either hope or faith, for clearly they anticipated ministering to a deceased body. They did not expect to experience a resurrection. Perhaps they were unaware of the preparation for burial done by Joseph and Nicodemus on Friday afternoon, or perhaps they had concluded that additional attention was needed.

Only Matthew records that an earthquake had taken place (Matt. 28:2). He recorded in 27:51 that an earthquake had opened the graves of deceased saints. Supposedly this second event was for the purpose of removing the stone from the mouth of the tomb. It is not to be supposed, however, that the removal of the stone was to let Jesus out of the tomb, for the resurrection had already taken place. The mystery of the resurrection is underscored by the fact that the gospel writers nowhere describe the phenomenon of the resurrection. They describe only the empty tomb and the appearances of the risen Savior.

Note the fact that women were the first witnesses that the tomb was empty. This significant detail serves to emphasize the validity and credibility of the resurrection account, for the Jewish culture of the first century did not view the testimony of women as legally acceptable. If the story had been fabricated, only men would have been cited as witnesses.

Matthew mentioned two women, Mary Magdalene and "the other Mary," the mother of James and Joseph (28:1; see 27:56), as the ones who went to the tomb. Mark records that Salome was with them (Mark 16:1). Note that the women went to the tomb to carry out the anointing while the men were not to be found.

Arriving at the tomb, they found that an angelic messenger had preceded them. Matthew tells us that it was the angel who had rolled the stone away. Mark described him as "a young man" (Mark 16:5). Luke

Jewish Burial Practices and Jesus' Tomb

Jewish tradition has seen proper burial to be of major importance. When death occurred, the eyes of the deceased were closed, the mouth was bound closed, and the body was washed and anointed. Since the climate in the Middle East is warm, and since the Jews did not embalm, a speedy burial was necessary. Spices were used to counter the problem of decomposition. The deceased would be buried in their own clothes or with specially prepared cloth wrappings. Occasionally coffins were used. Burial was in the ground or in a cave-like tomb.

Jesus' body was placed in a new tomb (Matt. 27:60). As with the burial practices of the day, the tomb would have been closed with a large circular rock.

Two sites in Jerusalem are pointed out today as the possible place of Jesus' burial. One is located in the Church of the Holy Sepulchre and enclosed by a shrine first built in perhaps the early fourth century. So much of the hillside has been removed by early masons and pilgrims that very little of the original features remain. In the 1800s a second site, known as Gordon's Calvary, was suggested. The tomb has an entry chamber and a place for one body to be interred. However, debate continues over the precise location of the empty tomb of Jesus.

added that a second angel was present (Luke 24:4). Note that each account furnishes further details. The gospel writers speak of "like lightning" and "clothing as white as snow," certainly appropriate descriptions of God's messenger (Matt. 28:3).

The Message of the Angel (28:5–8)

Recognizing that the women were understandably terrified because of what they saw, the angel said, "Do not be afraid" (28:5). Quite literally, the meaning is, *stop being afraid*. He acknowledged their anticipated task of anointing Jesus' body, but he gave them a splendid, ringing declaration, "He is not here, for He has risen, just as He said" (28:6). He further invited them to confirm that Jesus was alive again, instructing them, "Come see the place where He was lying" (28:6). They had indeed come to the right place, but instead of a lifeless body they found an empty tomb.

Can you image their conversation as they finished their task, placed Jesus' body in Joseph's tomb, and sealed the tomb with the stone?

The women were given the thrilling assignment of being the first human messengers to declare the resurrection of Jesus. "Tell His disciples," said the angel (28:7). "Go quickly" was his command (28:7). No doubt their feet grew wings as they flew to tell the Eleven of the astonishing good news.

Their message included instructions that the Eleven were to meet the risen Lord in Galilee (28:7). The emphasis on the last and triumphant meeting in Galilee seems to focus on Matthew's tendency to view that province as the place of acceptance and victory. Jerusalem had been the place of rejection and death, of betrayal and crucifixion. Galilee had been the site of Jesus' first miracle and the area where his most extensive ministry had taken place. All the Twelve were from Galilee except Judas, and there the crowds had thronged to hear Jesus' teachings.

The hurried departure of the women to tell the wonderful news is described in seemingly contradictory terms, "with fear and great joy" (28:8). Yet in the light of what they had just experienced, how fitting the antithetical emotions are. "Fear" no doubt characterized their being confronted by an angelic messenger from heaven. Who would not be terrified by seeing the dazzling appearance and by hearing from one described as "an angel of the Lord" (28:2)? "Joy" described their response to the

147

Application Actions

- Consider the implications of the resurrection of Jesus in the life of the believer. Find New Testament passages that focus on these implications (see, for example, 1 Corinthians 15).
- Contrast the empty tomb of Jesus with the burial places of founders of other world religions.

completely unexpected declaration that the One whom they thought was dead and buried was truly and vibrantly alive.

Should we as twenty-first century Christians not share the message of our risen Savior with the same emotions? We are fearful for unsaved friends and loved ones who face a tragic destiny without Christ. We are fearful of the consequences that are ours if we fail to warn the lost and, as the Lord reminded Ezekiel, have blood on our hands (Ezekiel 33:7–9). Yet we have great joy because we know from experience the redemptive grace of our Lord. We know the message we have to declare can transform lives and nations and cultures.

The Appearance of the Lord (28:9–10)

As the women ran to carry their thrilling report to the Eleven, they had a startling experience. Although they had seen an empty tomb and an angelic messenger, they now were suddenly confronted by the living Lord himself. The tense of the verb itself may well connote the idea of suddenness. Take notice of Jesus' greeting to the women (28:9). The King James Version translates the greeting, "All hail," while the New International Version reads, "Greetings." The term is not nearly as formal as it may seem. No fanfare or dramatic tone is involved, for Jesus simply said *hello* or perhaps *good morning*. In other words, Jesus spoke to them in a perfectly natural way. This in itself underscores the credibility of the account.

The gospel is for everyone.

Matthew records that they "took hold of His feet and worshiped Him" (28:9). Their posture indicates reverence and worship. Does this say something about the nature of Jesus' resurrected body? He was not a phantom or an apparition but rather so real that he could be touched.

148

Jesus reiterated the words of the angelic messenger about the meeting in Galilee, this time as a command. He instructed the Eleven to go into Galilee to meet him (28:10). This meeting, described later in chapter 28, was to be an occasion when Jesus would give significant final marching orders to the Eleven.

Then came Sunday morning! . . . Women were the first witnesses that the tomb was empty.

Matthew 28:11–15 records the activities of the soldiers who had guarded the tomb of Jesus. How much they saw is not clear. It is evident that they knew the tomb was empty and that they had failed to keep the tomb secure. Very probably the soldiers were Romans but placed by Pilate at the disposal of the Jewish religious leaders (27:62–66). Consequently, they went to the chief priests to report their failure. Rather than investigating the situation to determine the facts, the priests bribed the soldiers to lie. Matthew recorded that "a large sum of money" (28:12) was involved and that the soldiers were to report that Jesus' friends stole the body while they were asleep (28:13). Of course, sleeping on guard duty has always had disastrous consequences, and so the chief priests agreed to persuade Pilate and "'keep you out of trouble'" (28:14).

The Meeting in Galilee (28:16–20)

Following the command of Jesus, the Eleven went to Galilee to meet him. Matthew wrote that they met Jesus at "the mountain" (28:16). The definite article is in the Greek text. Which mountain? The mountain where the Sermon on the Mount was delivered? Some other significant mountain? We do not know. However, mountaintops have often been involved in unique revelation throughout Scripture.

The women were given the thrilling assignment of being the first human messengers to declare the resurrection of Jesus.

The statement, "but some were doubtful," is intriguing (28:17). Who were these? Why did they doubt? The verb used here speaks more of uncertainty and hesitation than of unbelief. Remember, they were standing in the presence of One who had been crucified, pronounced dead, and buried in a rock tomb. No doubt theirs was the doubt of amazement, realizing that that they were seeing something patently supernatural.

149

Jesus claimed "all authority" in heaven and earth (28:18). Jesus had authority during his earthly ministry, but now in the light of his resurrection he spoke of "all authority" being his. We must affirm that as the Son of God and the agent of creation, all authority has always been his.

Should we as twenty-first century Christians not share the message of our risen Savior . . . ?

Perhaps the expression is parallel to Paul's statement in Romans that Jesus has been "declared" or proven to be the Son of God with power by the resurrection of the dead (Romans 1:4).

The Great Commission of Jesus is found in Matthew 28:19–20. The two verses contain three participles—"going . . . baptizing . . . teaching"—and an imperative verb, "make disciples." The one strong command to make disciples, however, carries over to the participles. The result is that Jesus requires all four of these activities of his followers:

- We are to *go*. For some this means across the street, and for others it means across the seas.
- We are to *make disciples*. Our fundamental task is to use our influence and our words to share the good news of a risen Savior, leading individuals to exercise faith in Jesus Christ.
- We are to *baptize*. Leading a person to a public declaration of his or her decision to follow Christ is part of the responsibility. Remember that in the first Christian century baptism was what we today often call a "public profession of faith."
- We are to *teach*. Nurturing the new Christian and providing the means for him or her to grow to spiritual maturity is an essential part of evangelism. The infinitive ("to observe") used with this fourth admonition deserves attention (28:20). It means *to keep watch over, to protect*, in the sense of protecting, preserving, guarding. The implication is that the new believer is to obey Christ's commands and then pass them on to others.

The term "nations" (28:19) is a translation of the regular Greek word for Gentiles. Some interpreters consequently conclude that this excludes Jewish people from the mission given to the disciples. But to send the disciples to the Gentiles was to expand the scope of the gospel message. Now participation in the kingdom will be based not on race but on one's relationship with the risen Lord. The gospel is for everyone.

QUESTIONS

1. What significance do you see in the fact that the first appearance of Jesus after his resurrection was to women?

2. Using your imagination and the first several paragraphs of this lesson as a starting point, what do you think Joseph of Arimathea and Nicodemus said to each other as they completed the preparation of Jesus' body for burial?

3. What arguments have you heard that attempt to explain away the empty tomb and Jesus' resurrection? How would you counter them?

4. What is the basis for your belief in the resurrection of Jesus?

GALATIANS: By Grace Through Faith and EPHESIANS: God's Plan and Our Response

UNIT ONE, PROCLAIMING THE WAY OF FAITH

UNIT TWO, LIVING THE WAY OF FAITH

UNIT THREE, GOD'S INTENTION FOR US

UNIT FOUR, LIVING OUT GOD'S INTENTION

GALATIANS: By Grace Through Faith and
EPHESIANS: God's Plan and Our Response[1]

Andrew T. Lincoln. *Ephesians*. Word Biblical Commentary. Volume 42. Dallas, Texas: Word Books, Publisher, 1990.

John William MacGorman. *Galatians*. The Broadman Bible Commentary. Volume 11. Nashville, Tennessee: Broadman Press, 1971.

Ralph P. Martin. *Ephesians*. The Broadman Bible Commentary. Volume 11. Nashville, Tennessee: Broadman Press, 1971.

Leon Morris. *Galatians: Paul's Charter of Christian Freedom*. Downers Grove: InterVarsity Press, 1996.

Curtis Vaughan. *Galatians: A Study Guide Commentary*. Grand Rapids: Zondervan, 1972.

NOTES

1. Listing a book does not imply full agreement by the writers or BAPTISTWAY with all of its comments.

Announcing Beliefs Important to Baptists

Beliefs Important to Baptists is a series of undated Bible studies on who Baptists are and what they believe. These lessons can be used in various settings—such as in an adult Sunday School class, in a Discipleship Training study, as a Wednesday evening study, or in a new member class. *Beliefs Important to Baptists* is produced in four different studies. Each study contains member lessons and a teacher's edition. The teacher's edition contains both the member lessons and suggestions for teaching. Plan to study all the lessons in *Beliefs Important to Baptists*! (They can be studied in any order.)

Who in the World Are Baptists, Anyway?

A Bible study lesson that summarizes basic biblical understandings about who Baptists are, what they believe, and how they live.

Bible comments are by **Bill Pinson, Jr.**, Executive Director Emeritus of the Baptist General Convention of Texas. Teaching suggestions are by **Robby Barrett**, minister of education, First Baptist Church, Amarillo.

Beliefs Important to Baptists: I

This four-session unit provides a study of these key beliefs of Baptists:
- The Authority of the Bible
- Believer's Baptism and Church Membership
- Congregational Church Government
- Evangelism and Missions

Bible comments are by **Ebbie Smith**, pastor, Garden Acres Baptist Church, Burleson, and retired professor of Christian Ethics and Missions, Southwestern Baptist Theological Seminary. Teaching suggestions are by **Robby Barrett**, First, Amarillo.

Beliefs Important to Baptists: II

This four-session unit provides a study of these key beliefs of Baptists:
- Salvation Only by Grace Through Faith
- Soul Competency and the Priesthood of the Believer
- Baptism and the Lord's Supper
- The Autonomy of the Local Congregation

Bible comments are by **Rosalie Beck**, professor in the religion department at Baylor University. Teaching suggestions are by **Deborah McCollister**, professor of English, Dallas Baptist University.

Beliefs Important to Baptists: III

This four-session unit provides a study of these key beliefs of Baptists:
- The Deity and Lordship of Jesus Christ
- The Security of the Believer
- Voluntary Cooperation Among Churches
- Religious Freedom and Separation of Church and State

Bible comments are by **James Semple**, director, State Missions Commission, Baptist General Convention of Texas. Teaching suggestions are by **Larry Shotwell**, minister of adult education, First Baptist Church, San Angelo.

To order *Beliefs Important to Baptists*, use the order form in this issue of *Bible Study for Texas*.

How to Order More Bible Study Materials

It's easy! Just fill in the following information. Note that for *Bible Study for Texas* a Large Print edition of the *Study Guide* is available beginning with this issue. Note also that beginning with this issue the *Teaching Guide* includes additional Bible comments for teachers.

Title of item	Price	Quantity	Cost
This Issue:			
Matthew: Jesus As the Fulfillment of God's Promises—Study Guide	$1.95	_____	_____
Matthew: Jesus As the Fulfillment of God's Promises—Large Print Study Guide	$1.95	_____	_____
Matthew: Jesus As the Fulfillment of God's Promises—Teaching Guide	$2.45	_____	_____
Already Available:			
God's Message in the Old Testament— Study Guide	$1.95	_____	_____
God's Message in the Old Testament—Teaching Guide	$1.95	_____	_____
Luke: Meeting Jesus Again, Anew—Study Guide	$1.95	_____	_____
Luke: Meeting Jesus Again, Anew—Teaching Guide	$1.95	_____	_____
Acts: Sharing God's Good News with Everyone—Study Guide	$1.95	_____	_____
Acts: Sharing God's Good News with Everyone—Teaching Guide	$1.95	_____	_____
Romans: Good News for a Troubled World—Study Guide	$1.95	_____	_____
Romans: Good News for a Troubled World— Teaching Guide	$1.95	_____	_____
Coming for use beginning June 2001			
Galatians: By Grace Through Faith, and Ephesians: God's Plan and Our Response—Study Guide	$1.95	_____	_____
Galatians: By Grace Through Faith, and Ephesians: God's Plan and Our Response— Large Print Study Guide	$1.95	_____	_____
Galatians: By Grace Through Faith, and Ephesians:God's Plan and Our Response— Teaching Guide	$2.45	_____	_____
Coming for use beginning September 2001			
God's Message in the New Testament—Study Guide	$1.95	_____	_____
God's Message in the New Testament— Large Print Study Guide	$1.95	_____	_____
God's Message in the New Testament— Teaching Guide	$2.45	_____	_____

Beliefs Important to Baptists

Who in the World Are Baptists, Anyway? (one lesson)	$ .45	_____	_____
Who in the World Are Baptists, Anyway?— Teacher's Edition	$ .55	_____	_____
Beliefs Important to Baptists: I (four lessons)	$1.35	_____	_____
Beliefs Important to Baptists: I—Teacher's Edition	$1.75	_____	_____
Beliefs Important to Baptists: II (four lessons)	$1.35	_____	_____
Beliefs Important to Baptists: II—Teacher's Edition	$1.75	_____	_____
Beliefs Important to Baptists: III (four lessons)	$1.35	_____	_____
Beliefs Important to Baptists: III—Teacher's Edition	$1.75	_____	_____

*Charges for standard shipping service:	
Subtotal up to $20.00	$3.95
Subtotal $20.01—$50.00	$4.95
Subtotal $50.01—$100.00	10% of subtotal
Subtotal $100.01 and up	8% of subtotal

For express shipping service:
Call 1–800–355–5285
for information on additional charges.
Please allow at least three weeks for standard delivery.

Subtotal _____

Shipping* _____

TOTAL _____

Number of FREE copies of *Brief Basics for Texas Baptists* needed for leading adult Sunday School department periods _____

Your name

Your church

Mailing address

City   State   Zip code

MAIL this form with your check for the total amount to
Bible Study/Discipleship Division
Baptist General Convention of Texas
333 North Washington
Dallas, TX 75246–1798
(Make checks to "Baptist General Convention of Texas.")

OR, **FAX** your order anytime to: 214–828–5187, and we will bill you.

OR, **CALL** your order toll-free: 1–800–355–5285
(8:30 a.m.–5:00 p.m., M-F), and we will bill you.

OR, **E-MAIL** your order to our internet e-mail address:
baptistway@bgct.org, and we will bill you.

We look forward to receiving your order! Thank you!